Ketogenic Instant Pot & Meal Prep – 2 books in 1

Discover over 100 Easy, Delicious, and Healthy Recipes for beginners, plus The essential 30 Days Ketogenic Meal prep.

Written By

Allyson C. Naquin

&

Alicia J. Taylor

Contents

Ketogenic Diet Instant Pot

100 Easy, Delicious, and Healthy Recipes to Cook in the Pressure Cooker

Written by

Allyson C. Naquin

Introduction

Congratulations on downloading your personal copy of *Ketogenic Diet Instant Pot*. Thank you for doing so.

The following chapters will provide you 100 recipes, and information on the benefits of the ketogenic diet.

There are plenty of books on this subject on the market, thanks again for choosing this one! Every effort was made to ensure it is full of as much useful information as possible. Please enjoy!

Congratulations on downloading your personal copy of *Ketogenic Diet Instant Pot*. Thank you for doing so.

The Ketogenic Diet

A popular low-carb diet, the keto diet works by keeping your body in a state of ketosis where it produces ketones that are used for energy. Foods that are high in carbs cause the body to produce glucose and insulin.

Because glucose gets used for energy, the fat that's consumed isn't used and is stored. With a diet high in carbs, the body will continue to use glucose for energy. As you lower your carb intake, the body will reach ketosis.

Ketosis happens whenever food consumption becomes low in order to help the person live. During this state, the body produces ketones that the liver produces to break fats down. The purpose of the keto diet is to force the body to enter this state, but this isn't done by starving our self. It's done by starving the body of carbohydrates.

Adding the use of an Instant Pot only makes it easier to reap all of the benefits of the keto diet. The Instant Pot will make cooking your meals easier and healthier. You could probably also take you favorite keto recipes you have and change them to be cooked in the Instant Pot if you want. The Instant Pot just makes life easier when it comes to cooking, so let's look at the benefits it can help you receive.

Weight Loss

When on a keto diet, you get your energy from your body fat, so you are going to start losing weight. Your insulin level is going to drop significantly, and this makes the body burn more fat.

Past research has discovered that a keto diet will provide better results than a low-fat, high-carb diet, and this is true for long-term results as well.

A lot of keto dieters will drink ketoproof coffee in the morning to add more MCT oils to their diet, which you can get from coconut oil or by purchasing MCT oil. This is will fat loss and produces more ketones.

Cholesterol and Blood Pressure

This diet will also improve your cholesterol and triglyceride levels that are connected to a buildup in the arteries. When compared to a diet that is low in fat, a low-carb diet will raise HDL levels and lower LDL levels.

Most of the research into low-carb diets found that they have shown better improvement in blood pressure levels than other types of diets. Excessive weight is connected to blood pressure, so this makes the keto diet a bonus because it helps you to lose weight.

Before you dive into this diet, you will need to make a plan. A number of carbs you consume will be dependent on the amount of weight you want to lose and how fast you want to lose it. The lower the number of net carbs you consume, the faster you are going to lose weight.

You will have to limit the number of carbs found in all types of foods. You shouldn't eat refined sugars that are found in fruit, wheat, legumes, bread, beans, pasta, potatoes, cereals, and starch. There are expectations, such as avocado, star fruits, and berries.

The keto diet is a diet that is low in carbs, moderate in proteins, and high in fats. This means that your calories should break down with 70% coming from fats, 25% coming from protein, and 5% from carbs.

You should start out at 20 to 30 net carbs per day, but you can reduce the number further if you are looking to lose weight faster, but not too fast. You will want to keep track of your macros.

To figure out your net carbs, you take the total carb amount and subtract the dietary fiber amount. This means if a food has a total carb amount of 30 and a dietary fiber content of 26, then the net carb amount is going to be 4 net carbs.

Now, once you start the diet, actually reaching ketosis is fairly simple. You reach ketosis by restricting your carb intake to around 20 grams of net carbs per day. You also need to limit your protein. You can have more protein than carbs, but too much can slow your ketosis because the body can change it to glucose.

There's no need to worry about your fat intake; your body is just going to burn that and will need it for energy. This ensures that you won't enter starvation mode.

Keep yourself hydrated and drink plenty of water. This will help with hunger and regulate normal bodily functions.

You may develop the keto flu as well. This will mimic the regular flu where you will feel lethargic, tired, nauseated, and unmotivated. This will normally only happen in the first week or two and shouldn't last more than a few days. It goes away once your body becomes used to the keto diet. Increase your water and salt intake can also lessen the symptoms.

Now I believe you are ready to move onto the tasty recipes that you can fix quickly in your Instant Pot.

Main Dishes

1. Easy Balsamic Pot Roast

Serves: 10

Prep: 5 minutes

Ingredients:

Parsley, chopped – garnish

¼ tsp xanthan gum

1 tsp garlic powder

½ c onion, chopped

2 c water

3 lb boneless chuck roast

¼ c balsamic vinegar

1 tsp pepper

1 tbsp kosher salt

Directions:

Slice your roast in half and season it with the garlic, pepper, and salt. Set your pot to sauté and brown up the roast,

Place the onion, water, and balsamic vinegar. Place the lid and seal it. Set it to manual and cook for 35 minutes. Once done, quick release the pressure and remove the lid.

Carefully take the meat and chunk it up and get rid of any large pieces of fat.

Set the pot back on sauté, and let the mixture in the pot start to boil. Let it cook for around ten minutes. Mix the xanthan gum and mix the meat back in. Turn the heat off and serve on top of cauliflower with some fresh parsley.

Nutrition Information per Serving:

Calories: 393 Protein: 30g Carbohydrates: 3g net Fat: 28g

2. Unstuffed Cabbage Roll Soup

Serves: 9

Prep: 15 minutes

Ingredients:

5 c beef broth

½ tsp oregano

1 tsp salt

2 c riced cauliflower

16 oz marinara sauce

1 tsp pepper

8 c sliced cabbage

2 lb ground beef

½ c shallots, chopped

2 tbsp EVOO

½ c onion, chopped

1 tsp parsley

2 minced garlic cloves

Directions:

Set your Instant Pot to sauté and place the garlic and olive oil until fragrant. Mix the shallots and onions and cook until they become soft.

Mix the ground beef and allow it to brown. Mix the marinara sauce and all the seasonings. Stir well until the beef is coated.

Stir in the cauliflower, and make sure it is coated with the beef mixture.

Mix the cabbage and the beef broth and place the lid into place.

Set the Instant Pot to slow cook for three hours. Take the lid off once done and stir everything together before serving.

Nutrition Information per Serving:

Calories: 312 Protein: 31.1g Carbohydrates: 9.8g net Fat: 15.2g

3. Chili

Serves: 10

Prep: 10 minutes

Ingredients:

1 bay leaf

2 tbsp Worcestershire sauce

2 15 oz can diced tomatoes

1 tbsp oregano

6 oz can tomato paste

2 tbsp cumin

1 tsp pepper

8 garlic cloves, minced

2 tsp sea salt

½ large onion, chopped

4 oz can green chilies

¼ c chili powder

2 ½ lb ground beef

Directions:

Set your Instant Pot to the sauté setting. Mix the onion and let it cook for five to seven minutes, or until they become translucent. Mix the garlic until it becomes fragrant, don't let it burn.

Add the beef, and cook. This will take about eight to ten minutes.

Stir all the other ingredients, except for the bay leaf, until well combined. Nestle the bay leaf into the middle of the mixture, but do not stir.

Place the lid on and lock it into place. Stop the sauté cycle and set it to the meat/stew setting and cook for 35 minutes.

Allow the pressure to release naturally. Take out the bay leaf, and stir everything together again. Enjoy.

Nutrition Information per Serving:

Calories: 393 Protein: 23g Carbohydrates: 10g net Fat: 18g

4. Pork Ribs

Serves: 6

Prep: 10 minutes

Ingredients:

5 lbs of pork ribs, country style

Rub:

1 tsp onion powder

1 tsp paprika

½ tsp allspice

1 ½ tbsp kosher salt

½ tsp pepper

1 tbsp erythritol

½ tsp ground coriander

1 tsp garlic powder

Sauce:

¼ tsp xanthan gum

½ tsp onion powder

½ tbsp allspice

½ tbsp ground mustard

2 tbsp red wine vinegar

¼ tsp liquid smoke

½ c water

2 tbsp erythritol

½ c ketchup

Directions:

Mix all of the dry rub ingredients together and rub it into the ribs. Coating them all very well.

Place the ribs in the Instant Pot, stacking them on top of each other.

Mix together the onion powder, allspice, mustard, liquid smoke, water, vinegar, sweetener, and ketchup. Make sure everything is whisked together.

Pour the mixture into the pot over the ribs.

Place the lid on and seal it into place. Set to manual and for 35 minutes at high pressure.

Once it is done, release all of the pressure and take off the lid.

Set the ribs out onto a plate.

Whisk the xanthan gum into the sauce mixture and set the pot to sauté and let it thicken for ten minutes. Serve the sauce over the ribs.

Nutrition Information per Serving:

Calories: 387 Protein: 27g Carbohydrates: 2g net Fat: 29g

5. Chicken

Serves: 10

Prep: 10 minutes

Ingredients:

6 garlic cloves, peeled

1 tsp paprika

2 tbsp lemon juice

¼ tsp pepper

1 tbsp coconut oil

1 ½ c bone broth

1 tsp thyme

4 lb whole chicken

½ tsp sea salt

Directions:

Mix together the pepper, salt, thyme, and paprika together. Rub this mixture all over the chicken.

Add the coconut oil in the Instant Pot. Allow it to cook until it starts to simmer. Set the chicken in the pot with the breast down for six to seven minutes.

Flip the chicken and add the garlic cloves, broth, and lemon juice.

Place the lid and lock it into place. Set the pot to high. Set to 25 minutes.

Once done, release the pressure.

Ease the chicken out of the pot and allow it to sit for five minutes before you serve it.

Nutrition Information per Serving:

Calories: 413 Protein: 32.6g Carbohydrates: .7g net Fat: 30.2g

6. Lamb Shanks

Serves: 4 to 6

Prep: 5 minutes

Ingredients:

1 tsp fish sauce

1 lb Roma tomatoes

2 medium carrots, chopped

1 large onion, chopped

3 garlic cloves, smashed

1/5 c minced parsley

1 tbsp tomato paste

1 c bone broth

1 tbsp balsamic vinegar

2 tbsp ghee, divided

Pepper

2 celery stalks, chopped

Salt

3 lb lamb shanks

Directions:

Season your lamb shanks with some pepper and salt. Set your Instant Pot to sauté and add the ghee. Place in the lamb shanks and sear.

As the lamb is searing in the pot, take this time to chop up all of your vegetables. Take the lamb out of your pot and set it to the side.

Put in the remaining ghee in. Place the celery, carrots, and onions in the pot and sprinkle with some pepper and salt.

After the veggies have softened up, add the garlic cloves and tomato paste and stir everything together for a minute.

Place the shanks back into the pot as well as the tomatoes. Add the balsamic vinegar, bone broth, and fish. Give it a little more fresh pepper, and then lock the lid into place. Set to manual on high pressure to cook for 50 minutes.

Once everything is done, quick release the pressure and remove the lid.

Adjust the sauce flavorings as needed, and serve the lamb covered in the sauce.

Nutrition Information per Serving:

Calories: 180 Protein: 7g Carbohydrates: 4g net Fat: 5g

7. Rotisserie Chicken

Serves: 4 to 6

Prep: 8 minutes

Ingredients:

1 ½ tsp salt

1 lemon, halved

1 tsp garlic powder

1 onion, quartered

½ tsp pepper

1 c chicken broth

1 whole chicken

1 tsp paprika

1 ¾ tbsp avocado oil

Directions:

Clean the chicken thoroughly and pat dry. Slide the onion and the lemon into the chicken's cavity.

Stir together all of the above spices, and then mix the oil. Mix until well incorporated.

Switch your Instant Pot to sauté mode. Rub half the spice mixture all over the top side of the chicken. Lay your chicken into the pot with the breast side down. Rub the remainder of the spice mixture on the other half of the chicken.

Let the chicken cook for three to four minutes. Carefully flip over the chicken, and let the skin on the bottom crisp.

Pour the chicken stock.

Set the lid on and lock into place. Set on high and let it cook for 25 minutes. Once done, release pressure.

Remove the lid and set out the chicken. Allow it to rest for five minutes.

Nutrition Information per Serving:

Calories: 180 Protein: 19g Carbohydrates: 0g net Fat: 12g

8. Pork Chops

Serves: 5

Prep: 5 minutes

Ingredients:

4-6 boneless pork chops

1 c water

1 stick butter

1 package ranch mix

1 tbsp coconut oil

Directions:

Set the cooker to sauté and add the coconut oil to the pot. Brown chops. Add the butter and then sprinkle the ranch packet.

Pour the water and place the lid on and lock in place. Set to manual for five minutes.

Let pressure release, then pour over the buttery mix.

Nutrition Information per Serving:

Calories: 300 Protein: 27g Carbohydrates: 4g net Fat: 16g

9. Broccoli Cheese Soup

Serves: 4 to 6

Prep: 3 minutes

Ingredients:

4 c chicken stock

¼ tsp garlic powder

1 tsp pepper

1 c shredded carrots

1 c heavy cream

1 bunch broccoli, florets only

1 tsp salt

1 tbsp onion powder

2 c cheddar cheese

2 tbsp butter

Directions:

Set the cooker to sauté and add the butter until hot. Place all the ingredients except cheese and heavy cream. Place the lid on and lock into place.

Set on high for five minutes. Release pressure and mix the cheese and cream. Enjoy.

Nutrition Information per Serving:

Calories: 92 Protein: 7.3g Carbohydrates: 8g net Fat: 2.2g

10. Crack Chicken

Serves: 6

Prep: 5 minutes

Ingredients:

¼ tsp xanthan gum

1 packet ranch seasoning

2 lb chicken breast

4 oz cheddar cheese

8 oz cream cheese

6-8 slices bacon, cooked

Directions:

Place the chicken and cream cheese and sprinkle with the ranch seasoning. Add a cup of water and set on high for 25 minutes.

Release the pressure and shred the chicken. Then, set the pot to sauté and mix the xanthan gum, chicken, and cheese. Mix the bacon and enjoy.

Nutrition Information per Serving:

Calories: 540 Protein: 46g Carbohydrates: 8g net Fat: 46g

11.Chicken Wings

Serves: 2-3

Prep: 5 minutes

Ingredients:

½ c BBQ sauce

2 lb chicken wings

Directions:

Add a cup of water to your pot and set in a steamer basket. Place the wings, then lock the lid and cook on high for five minutes. Once done, naturally release the pressure. Remove the chicken and toss the barbecue sauce.

Nutrition Information per Serving:

Calories: 150 Protein: 10g Carbohydrates: 2g net Fat: 14g

12. Italian Beef

Serves: 12 cups

Prep: 5 minutes

Ingredients:

6 portobello mushrooms

1 tsp onion powder

2 tbsp Dijon

¼ tsp pepper

2 ½ lb chuck roast

1 tsp rosemary

½ c water

1 tsp basil

1 tsp oregano

1 tsp garlic powder

¼ tsp salt

1 tbsp red wine vinegar

Directions:

Mix the spice together and rub on the roast. Add the oil and place to sauté and sear the roast. Add the vinegar and water. Set to slow cook for 7-8 hours. Take out the beef and shred.

Skim off the fat and mix the Dijon, then stir the beef back in and serve on the mushrooms

Nutrition Information per Serving:

Calories: 410 Protein: 30g Carbohydrates: 6g net Fat: 24g

13. Beef Short Ribs

Serves: 4 to 6

Prep: 5 minutes

Ingredients:

3 cloves minced garlic

¼ tsp xanthan gum

2 tbsp tomato paste

2 tbsp olive oil

½ c dry red wine

1 large chopped onion

2 slices bacon, chopped

1 c beef broth

4 large beef short ribs

Directions:

Season the ribs with pepper and salt. Put oil in the Instant Pot and Set the cooker to sauté. Once the oil is hot, brown the ribs in batches. Place on the plate until all the ribs have been browned.

Add the bacon to the Instant Pot and cook until crispy. Add onion and cook until soft, then mix the garlic in until it is fragrant.

Mix in wine and deglaze the pot. Place the tomato paste and beef broth and mix, then place the ribs.

Close the lid and seal, then set on high for 40 minutes. When done, naturally release the pressure for ten minutes and quick release any remaining.

Remove the ribs and place on the plate. Cover with foil to keep warm. Strain juices to remove any fat, then return to the pot.

Add xanthan gum to juices. Set the cooker to sauté and allow to boil. Stir until juices thicken, then turn off the pot.

Add the ribs and toss to coat. Put the lid on and allow the ribs to absorb sauce for ten minutes. Stir to coat.

Have with cauliflower.

Nutrition Information per Serving:

Calories: 820.8 Protein: 93.1g Carbohydrates: 4.6g net Fat: 43.1g

14. Beef Stew

Serves: 4

Prep: 5 minutes

Ingredients:

1 sliced onion

3 c beef broth

2 bay leaves

2 tbsp olive oil

6 sprigs thyme

4 cloves garlic

4 carrots, peeled and sliced

2 lbs. beef stew meat

1 c water

1 tbsp tomato paste

Directions:

Season the meat with pepper and salt. Add oil and Set the cooker to sauté. When the oil is hot, brown the meat for about five minutes. Do this in two batches.

Once the beef is browned, add carrots, garlic, and onion. Sauté a bit. Add thyme sprigs, bay leaves, tomato paste, and broth.

Close and seal the lid. Set on high. When Instant Pot starts to release steam, set the timer for 25 minutes. Naturally release the pressure, then take off the lid. Adjust seasonings as you see fit.

Nutrition Information per Serving:

Calories: 392 Protein: 54g Carbohydrates: 6g net Fat: 17g

15. Chicken and Broth

Serves: 6 to 8

Prep: 5 minutes

Ingredients:

10 c water

4 lb. chicken

1 chopped onion

2 tsp salt

1 tbsp black peppercorns

2 sliced celery stalks

2 bay leaves

3 carrots, peeled and sliced

2 tbsp olive oil

Directions:

Set the cooker on sauté and pour the oil and heat. Once hot, cook carrots, onion, and celery for five minutes.

Add the chicken breast side down. Add bay leaves, peppercorns, and salt. You can add any fresh herbs and seasonings of your choice here. Add water to cover chicken.

Close and seal the lid, the set on high. When it begins to release steam, set the timer for 35 minutes. Naturally release the pressure and take off the lid.

Remove the chicken and take the meat off the bone.

Serve as you like.

Nutrition Information per Serving:

Calories: 472 Protein: 36g Carbohydrates: 10g net Fat: 32g

16. Pork Roast with Mushroom Gravy

Serves: 9

Prep: 11 minutes

Ingredients:

4 c chopped cauliflower

1 tsp salt

1 medium onion, chopped

8 oz. portobello mushrooms, sliced

2 ribs celery

½ tsp black pepper

3 lb. pork roast

4 cloves garlic

2 c water

2 tbsp coconut oil

Directions:

Put water, celery, garlic, onion, and cauliflower in the bottom of the Instant Pot. Put the pork roast on top and season with pepper and salt.

Set to manual for 90 minutes if the roast is frozen and 60 minutes if thawed. Once done, quickly release the pressure.

Remove roast and put in the oven proof dish. Set the oven to 400 and cook while fixing gravy.

Place broth and vegetables in the blender. Blend until smooth, then set aside.

Set the cooker on sauté, then add the coconut oil and melt. Cook mushrooms until soft. Put blended veggies back into the Instant Pot and sauté until thick.

Serve over shredded pork.

Nutrition Information per Serving:

Calories: 521 Protein: 42g Carbohydrates: 7g net Fat: 36g

17. Egg Roll Soup

Serves: 6

Prep: 3minutes

Ingredients:

1 tsp ground ginger

1 tsp onion powder

1 tsp salt

2 c shredded carrots

½ head chopped cabbage

4 c beef broth

1 large diced onion

2/3 c coconut aminos

1 tsp garlic powder

1 tbsp olive oil

1 lb. ground pork

Directions:

Set the cooker on sauté, then pour the olive oil. When heated, add the pork. Once the pork is brown, add the onion and cook until pork is done.

Add the rest of the ingredients, then close and seal the lid. Set on high for 25 minutes then release the pressure.

Remove the lid and serve.

Nutrition Information per Serving:

Calories: 340 Protein: 18g Carbohydrates: 24g net Fat: 19g

18. Sausage and Peppers

Serves: 5

Prep: 5 minutes

Ingredients:

2 tsp garlic powder

1 15 oz. can tomato sauce

4 large bell peppers, cut into strips

1 c water

1 tbsp Italian seasoning

1 28 oz. can diced tomatoes

1 tbsp basil

2 19 oz. pkg. Italian sausage

Directions:

Place the Italian seasoning, garlic powder, basil, water, tomato sauce, and tomatoes into the Instant Pot. Put peppers on top. DO NOT MIX.

Close and seal the lid. Set on high for 25 minutes. Once done, release the pressure then open the lid. Serve and enjoy.

Nutrition Information per Serving:

Calories: 606 Protein: 31g Carbohydrates: 10g net Fat: 43g

19. Kalua Pork

Serves: 12

Prep: 5 minutes

Ingredients:

2 tsp salt

1 tbsp liquid smoke

½ c water

1 tbsp olive oil

4 lb pork butt

Directions:

Cut the pork butt in half. Set the cooker on sauté. Pour the oil and allow to heat. After it's hot, brown the pork. When both halves are browned, turn the pot off and add liquid smoke and water. Place roasts into the pot then sprinkle with salt.

Close and seal the lid. Set on high for 90 minutes. When timer sounds, naturally release the pressure for about 20 minutes. Remove the lid.

Take the meat out and shred. Throw away any fat. Add juices to the pot to keep the meat moist.

Serve over riced cauliflower.

Nutrition Information per Serving:

Calories: 415 Protein: 36g Carbohydrates: 0g net Fat: 30g

20. Ribs with Coleslaw

Serves: 4

Prep: 30 minutes

Ingredients:

Ribs:

½ tsp paprika

½ tsp dry mustard

2.5 lbs. baby back ribs

¾ tsp black pepper

1 tsp onion powder

½ tsp chili powder

½ tsp garlic powder

1 c favorite barbecue sauce

½ tsp salt

Coleslaw:

1 small head cabbage

¼ c apple cider vinegar

½ head red cabbage

2 shredded carrots

1 c mayonnaise

2 tbsp sweetener of choice

Pepper

Salt

Directions:

Make the rub for ribs: Mix chili powder, pepper, dry mustard, garlic powder, salt, paprika, and onion powder. Stir to combine.

Cut the ribs into pieces, so they will fit in the Instant Pot. Stacking is okay. Coat ribs with dry rub.

Add one inch of water to the bottom. Place a trivet inside. Stack ribs on the trivet. Close and seal the lid. Set on high for 15 minutes.

While the ribs are cooking make the coleslaw: Put cabbage and carrots in large bowl. In a smaller bowl, mix the pepper, salt, sweetener, apple cider vinegar, and mayonnaise. Stir well to combine. Pour over cabbage and stir well to coat. Refrigerate until serving.

When the ribs are done, quick release the pressure. Put ribs on a plate. Remove the trivet and discard the liquid.

Add some barbecue sauce to the bottom of the pot and add some ribs, more sauce, more ribs, repeat until all the ribs and the sauce have been used.

Close and seal the lid. Set on high and cook for ten minutes.

Quick release the pressure and put ribs on the serving plates. Serve with coleslaw and enjoy.

Nutrition Information per Serving:
Calories: 958 Protein: 37g Carbohydrates: 19g net Fat: 76g

21. Chicken Chili Verde

Serves: 6

Prep: 10 minutes

Ingredients:

Salt

1 tbsp whole cumin seed

1 medium onion

1 tbsp fish sauce

2 Serrano chilies, stem removed, rough chopped

½ c cilantro leaves

2 Anaheim peppers, seeds and stem removed, rough chopped

6 cloves garlic, peeled

2 poblano peppers, seeds and stem removed, rough chopped

4 tomatillos, husks removed, quartered

3 lb. bone-in skinless chicken thighs

Directions:

Place cumin, garlic, onion, peppers, tomatillos, and chicken in the Instant Pot. Sprinkle generously with salt. Heat on high until simmering. Close and seal the lid. Set on high and cook 15 minutes. Quick release the pressure.

Carefully remove the chicken and place on a plate. Add fish sauce and cilantro. Blend with immersion blender until as smooth as you like it. Taste and adjust seasoning if needed. Put the chicken back in the cause. You can shred chicken if you would like or leave pieces whole. Place in a bowl and add cilantro and lime wedge. Serve and enjoy.

Nutrition Information per Serving:

Calories: 297 Protein: 45g Carbohydrates: 8g net Fat: 9g

22. Fall Off the Bone Chicken

Serves: 10

Prep: 10 minutes

Ingredients:

6 cloves garlic

1 ½ c chicken broth

¼ tsp black pepper

½ tsp salt

1 tbsp coconut oil

1 whole 4 lb. chicken

1 tsp paprika

2 tbsp lemon juice

1 tsp thyme

Directions:

Mix pepper, salt, thyme, and paprika. Rub on the chicken.

Set the cooker on sauté and heat the oil. Place the chicken in the pot, breast side down. Cook for seven minutes. Quick release the pressure, then open the lid and turn the chicken over. Add broth, garlic, and lemon juice.

Close and seal the lid. Set on high for 25 minutes.

Naturally release the pressure, then carefully open and take out the chicken. Let it stand for five minutes before you cut into it.

Nutrition Information per Serving:

Calories: 413 Protein: 32.63g Carbohydrates: .689g net Fat: 30.2g

23. Butter Chicken

Serves: 10

Prep: 15 minutes

Ingredients:

½ c cilantro

2 tsp garlic powder

½ c sliced almond

2 heaping tsp garam masala

2 heaping tsp paprika

2 cans refrigerated coconut milk

2 c stewed tomatoes

2 tsp ground ginger

12 oz. tomato paste

1 ½ tsp cayenne pepper

2 heaping tsp turmeric

3 tsp salt

1 ½ large chopped onions

1 tbsp ghee

3 lb. boneless skinless chicken thighs, diced

Directions:

Set the cooker to sauté, the melt the ghee. Add onions and two teaspoons of salt. Cook until onions are soft.

Add cayenne, paprika, turmeric, ginger, and garlic. Mix well and cook until fragrant.

Add canned tomatoes and watery part of coconut milk. Mix well with spices. Scraping spices off the bottom.

Add the chicken and stir well to combine, then close and seal the lid.

Set to manual and cook for eight minutes. Quick release the pressure. Stir coconut cream, garam masala, three-quarters of the cilantro, and tomato paste. Stir well to combine. Taste and add more salt, if needed.

When done, top with sliced almonds and cilantro.

Nutrition Information per Serving:

Calories: 270 Protein: 21g Carbohydrates: 8g net Fat: 6g

24. Lemon and Olive Chicken

Serves: 8 **Prep:** 10 minutes

Ingredients:

For Marinade:

½ tsp pepper

4 tbsp olive oil

3 lemons, juiced

½ bunch parsley, chopped

2 sprigs fresh sage

1 tsp salt

3 sprigs rosemary

2 cloves chopped garlic

For Chicken:

3.5 oz. Kalamata olives

½ c dry white wine

1 whole chicken, cut into pieces

Directions:

Make marinade by chopping sage, parsley, rosemary, and garlic. Put in a bowl and add lemon juice, pepper, salt, and olive oil. Mix well and set to the side.

Remove skin from chicken. Put the chicken in zip top bag and cover with marinade. Let it sit for four hours.

Set the Instant Pot to sauté. Add the oil and brown the chicken. Set aside.

Add wine, deglaze, and cook until almost evaporated.

Add the chicken with the dark meat first and white meat on top.

Measure remaining marinade and add it to the Instant Pot. Close and seal the lid.

Set your pot to high for ten minutes. Once done, quick release the pressure. Take off the lid and remove the chicken.

Reduce liquid by half. Put the chicken back in and glaze all the pieces.

Take chicken back out and sprinkle with lemon slices, olives, and rosemary.

Tell guests that olives do still have pits.

Nutrition Information per Serving:

Calories: 343 Protein: 27.2g Carbohydrates: 16g net Fat: 19.2g

25.Chicken and Sausage Stew

Serves: 6

Prep: 10 minutes

Ingredients:

6 cloves garlic

¼ tsp black pepper

1 tsp thyme

2 c chicken broth

2 large carrots

½ tsp smoked paprika

1 bay leaf

1 tsp salt

3 bell peppers

2 stalks celery

¼ c parsley

1 medium white onion

6 c chopped tomatoes

½ tsp crushed red chili flakes

¼ tsp cayenne

1 tbsp coconut oil

1 lb. andouille sausage

1 lb. boneless, skinless chicken thighs

Directions:

Heat the coconut oil in the bottom of the Instant Pot and set on sauté setting. Add the sausage and chicken and cook through. While cooking, slice the onion and dice the bell peppers. Chop the celery and carrots. Take the meat out of the pot and save for later.

Cook the veggies in the bottom of the pot, stirring occasionally. Mince garlic and put in pan. Add chopped tomatoes and broth. Bring to simmer.

When the sausage and the chicken are cool enough to touch, slice them into bite-size pieces. Place them back into the pot with the spices. Mince parsley and place in the pot. Give the stew another stir and close and seal the lid. Turn to soup setting and cook ten minutes. Enjoy.

Nutrition Information per Serving:

Calories: 250 Protein: 27g Carbohydrates: 10g net Fat: 9g

27.Creamy Chicken and Broccoli

Serves: 4 to 6

Prep: 8 minutes

Ingredients:

½ tsp salt

4 oz. cream cheese, diced

1/8 tsp red pepper flakes

2 large boneless chicken breasts

1 tsp xanthan gum

1 tbsp dried parsley

½ tsp pepper

1 tbsp olive oil

3 c chopped broccoli

14 oz. chicken broth

1 c shredded cheddar cheese

½ c chopped onion

1 tbsp butter

Directions:

Pepper and salt chicken breasts. Set the cooker on sauté. Place the butter and oil to the pot. When melted, brown the chicken breasts and put on a plate.

Add onion to the pot and cook until tender. Stir parsley, red pepper flakes, pepper, salt, and chicken broth. Add the chicken breasts.

Cover and seal the lid. Set on high and cook for five minutes. When timer goes off, use quick pressure release. Place the chicken on cutting board and cut into pieces.

Select sauté and add shredded and cream cheese. Stir until cheese is melted.

Add the chicken and broccoli. Simmer for five minutes until chicken and broccoli are hot.

Serve over riced cauliflower.

Nutrition Information per Serving:

Calories: 180 Protein: 18g Carbohydrates: 14g net Fat: 4.5g

28. Kalua Pig

Serves: 8

Prep: 5 minutes

Ingredients:

3 slices bacon

1 c water

1 ½ tbsp. salt

5 peeled garlic cloves

1 cabbage, cored, cut into six wedges

5 lbs. bone-in pork shoulder roast

Directions:

Drape the bacon in the pot. Set the cooker to sauté and cook the bacon. Slice roast into three pieces. Cut some slits into pork and place in garlic.

Top with salt. Check the bacon and turn to brown both sides.

Set in pork and keep single meat layer then add water.

Seal the lid and set on high then cook for 90 minutes.

When timer goes off, use natural pressure release. When all pressure has been released, carefully open the lid and check to see of pork is tender.

Remove the meat and shred. Taste the remaining liquid in bottom and adjust seasonings if needed.

Add the wedges of cabbage to the cooking liquid. Close and seal the lid. Set on high and cook for five minutes. When cabbage is finished, quick release the pressure.

Serve the pork with cabbage on top.

Nutrition Information per Serving:

Calories: 250 Protein: 20g Carbohydrates: 0g net Fat: 19g

29.Pork Chops with Carrots

Serves: 6

Prep: 15 minutes

Ingredients:

1 cup baby carrots

¼ c butter

Salt

1 chopped onion

3 tbsp Worcestershire sauce

1 c vegetable broth

Pepper

4 thick bone in pork chops

Directions:

Season chops with pepper and salt. Set the Instant Pot to sauté and melt two tablespoons of butter. Cook the pork chops until browned on each side then put on a plate.

Melt the rest of the butter and let the onion and carrots cook. Place the Worcestershire sauce and broth. Return the pork chops to the pot.

Close and seal the lid. Set on high for 13 minutes. When the timer goes off, release the pressure. Take off the lid and carefully take out carrots and chops. Serve.

Nutrition Information per Serving:

Calories: 310 Protein: 24g Carbohydrates: 15g net Fat: 16g

30. Braised Beef Ribs

Serves: 4

Prep: 10 minutes

Ingredients:

Water

3 cloves garlic

1 onion, quartered

1 tbsp olive oil

Salt

4 lbs. beef short ribs

Directions:

Season the ribs with salt. Set the cooker on sauté. Pour the oil to the pot and heat up. Brown the ribs once hot.

When all the ribs have been browned, put them back in the pot. Add water, garlic, and onion. Set your pot to high for 35 minutes.

Once done, quick release the pressure. You can either pull meat from the bones or leave them as they are.

Nutrition Information per Serving:

Calories: 84 Protein: 8.7g Carbohydrates: 0g net Fat: 2g

31. Lamb Stew

Serves: 4

Prep: 10 minutes

Ingredients:

1 large onion

3 large carrots

3 tbsp broth

1 acorn squash

½ tsp salt

1 sprig rosemary

6 cloves garlic

1 bay leaf

2 lbs lamb stew meat

Directions:

Peel, seed, and cube acorn squash. Slice carrots into coins, then peel and cut onion in half then thinly slice.

Put all the ingredients in the Instant Pot. Close and seal the lid. Set on high for 35 minutes.

When the timer goes off, release the pressure. Carefully take off the lid.

Serve and enjoy.

Nutrition Information per Serving:

Calories: 277 Protein: 5.6g Carbohydrates: 14.6g net Fat: 18.6g

32. Texas Chili

Serves: 6

Prep: 10 minutes

Ingredients:

Pinch cumin

1 tsp garlic powder

½ tsp black pepper

26 oz. chopped tomatoes

4 tsp chili powder

4 large carrots, finely chopped

1 tbsp fresh parsley

1 tsp onion powder

1 tbsp Worcestershire sauce

1 tsp paprika

1 large diced onion

1 tsp salt

1 bell pepper, seeded and diced

1 lb. ground beef

Directions:

Set the Instant Pot to sauté, then add the beef and cook.

Add everything else and mix. Cover and seal the lid. Set to the cooker to meat and cook for 35 minutes.

When the chili is done, naturally release pressure. Remove the lid and serve

Nutrition Information per Serving:

Calories: 45 Protein: 7g Carbohydrates: 3g net Fat: 1.5g

33. Buffalo Chicken Soup

Serves: 2

Prep: 5 minutes

Ingredients:

½ c diced celery

1 tbsp ranch dressing mix

1 clove chopped garlic

¼ c diced onion

2 boneless skinless chicken breasts

2 c shredded cheddar cheese

2 tbsp butter

3 cups chicken broth

1/3 c hot sauce

1 c heavy cream

Directions:

Place all ingredients in the Instant Pot, except for the cheese and cream.

Close and seal the lid then set on high for ten minutes.

Once done, release the pressure.

Take out the chicken and shred, then mix back in. Add the cheese and cream. Stir to combine. Enjoy

Nutrition Information per Serving:

Calories: 130 Protein: 5g Carbohydrates: 12g net Fat: 6g

34. Lemon Garlic Chicken

Serves: 4

Prep: 10 minutes

Ingredients:

¼ c white cooking wine

¼ tsp paprika

1 tsp salt

1 tsp dried parsley

½ c chicken broth

3 to 4 tsp arrowroot flour

5 cloves minced garlic

1 large lemon juiced

1 tbsp ghee

1 diced onion

2 lbs. chicken breast

Directions:

Set the Instant Pot to sauté. Melt ghee. Cook the onion until soft. Mix everything else in, except arrowroot. Close and seal the lid.

Set on poultry. Make sure the steam valve is closed.

When done, quick release the pressure and remove the lid.

You can thicken the sauce by taking ¼ cup of the liquid from the pot and mix with the arrowroot flour, then add it back into the pot. Stir and serve.

Nutrition Information per Serving:

Calories: 216 Protein: 30.2g Carbohydrates: 7.3g net Fat: 6.7g

35. Olive Lemon Chicken

Serves: 6

Prep: 12 minutes

Ingredients:

¼ tsp xanthan gum

¾ c chicken broth

1 fennel bulb, chopped

12 chicken thighs

¼ tsp pepper

1 lemon, zest

¼ tsp salt

2 celery ribs, chopped

½ c parsley

½ tsp oregano

2 bay leaves

4 garlic cloves, crushed

16 green olives

1 onion, chopped

2 tbsp lemon juice

2 carrots, chopped

Directions:

Place the veggies and spices to your pot and set to chicken. Place the broth and ¾ cup of water. Close the lid and set on low for six hours.

Get rid of the bay leaves. Mix in the xanthan gum and the lemon juice. Place the lid and set the cooker for 15 minutes, until thickened. Stir the lemon zest and parsley. Enjoy.

Nutrition Information per Serving:

Calories: 350 Protein: 30g Carbohydrates: 6g net Fat: 16g

36. Pizza

Serves: 8

Prep: 20 minutes

Ingredients:

16 pepperoni slices

3 c spinach

3 c mozzarella

15 oz pizza sauce

¾ lb Italian sausage, cooked

¾ lb ground beef, cooked

Favorite topping

Directions:

Mix the onions, sauce, beef, and sausage together in your pot. Add half of the sauce and top with spinach, pepperoni, and half of your toppings and half of the mozzarella. Add the rest of the sauce and other ingredients, and lastly, the remaining half of the mozzarella. Close the lid, set to slow cook for 4-6 hours. Let cool, and cut into eight slices.

Nutrition Information per Serving:

Calories: 487 Protein: 30g Carbohydrates: 5.6g net Fat: 37g

International

37.Ropa Vieja

Serves: 6-8 **Prep:** 20 minutes

Ingredients:

1 tsp Goya Sazon

1 bay leaf

1 tsp cumin

½ tsp oregano

½ c chopped green olives

2 c sliced mild peppers

15 oz can diced tomatoes

1 c beef broth

½ c parsley, chopped

4 minced garlic cloves

2 tbsp vinegar

1 medium onion, sliced

Pepper and salt

2 lb flank steak

1 tbsp olive oil

Directions:

Generously season the flanks steak with some pepper and salt. Swirl the oil into the bottom of your Instant Pot and set it to sauté. Once it has heated, place the meat and brown both sides. Set it out on a plate to rest.

Place the onion and garlic and let it cook, mix the onions until soft. Mix the broth and deglaze the pot. Add bay leaf, cumin, oregano, peppers, tomatoes, and Goya Sazon. Nestle the flank steak into this mixture.

Lock the lid, then set your cooker to high pressure and cook for 40 minutes. Make sure you canceled the sauté mode before setting the cook time.

After the cooking time has finished, allow pressure to release. Open the lid and shred the meat. Remove the bay leaf, and stir the olives, vinegar, and parsley. Add as much pepper and salt as you need. Serve with cauliflower.

Nutrition Information per Serving: Calories: 249.5 Protein: 24.4g Carbohydrates: 8.4g net Fat: 11.6g

38. Goulash

Serves: 6-8

Prep: 5 minutes

Ingredients:

4 c beef stock

1 tbsp minced garlic

½ tsp hot paprika

2 cans petite diced tomatoes

2 tsp + 1 tsp olive oil

2 tbsp sweet paprika

1 large onion, sliced

1 large red bell pepper, sliced

1 ½ lb ground beef

Directions:

Set your Instant Pot to the sauté setting and add two teaspoons of oil and then place in the beef. Break it up as it browns. Once it's almost cooked, place the beef in a bowl with paper towels to drain.

As the meat is cooking, prepare your vegetables. Pour in remaining oil after you remove the beef and add the peppers and onions. Cook this until soft. Mix in hot paprika, garlic, and sweet paprika and let it cook for another couple of minutes. Make sure the paprika is cooked in with everything. You cannot skip this step.

Add stock and tomatoes, and Mix the beef. Place the lid and lock it into place. Set it to soup and cook for 15 minutes.

Once done, all the pressure to release naturally for a couple of minutes and the quick release the rest. Serve with some sour cream.

Nutrition Information per Serving:

Calories: 260 Protein: 25g Carbohydrates: 8 g net Fat: 12 g

39. Jamaican Jerk Pork

Serves: 12

Prep: 5 minutes

Ingredients:

½ c beef stock

1 tbsp olive oil

¼ c Jamaican Jerk spice blend, no sugar

4 lb pork shoulder

Directions:

Rub the oil over your roast and rub it down with the Jamaican Jerk seasoning.

Set your Instant Pot to sauté and set the meat to brown on all of the sides, then pour the beef broth.

Seal the lid into place and set the pot to high pressure on manual for 45 minutes.

Quick release the pressure and shred the meat and serve.

Nutrition Information per Serving:

Calories: 282 Protein: 23g Carbohydrates: 0g net Fat: 20g

40. No Noodle Lasagna

Serves: 8

Prep: 10 minutes

Ingredients:

8 oz. sliced mozzarella

1 lb. ground beef

½ cup Parmesan cheese

1 small onion. diced

1 25 oz. jar marinara sauce

1 large egg

2 cloves minced garlic

1 ½ cups ricotta cheese

Directions:

Set the Instant Pot to sauté. Brown ground beef with onion and garlic.

While meat is cooking, mix ricotta, parmesan, and egg in a bowl. Stir to combine.

Add marinara sauce to meat and mix well. Take out half of the meat.

Top the meat in the Instant Pot with half of the mozzarella cheese.

Spread half of the ricotta cheese over the mozzarella. Add the rest of the meat.

Add another layer of the mozzarella cheese and spread remaining ricotta cheese over that. Reserve some mozzarella for topping.

Close and seal the lid. Cook at high pressure for 10 minutes. Vent off steam, remove the lid, and add rest of mozzarella. Cover and allow the cheese to melt.

Serve and enjoy

Nutrition Information per Serving:

Calories: 339 Protein: 36g Carbohydrates: 6.3g net Fat: 3.2g

41. Italian Pot Roast

Serves: 8 to 10

Prep: 15 minutes

Ingredients:

1 jar sun dried tomatoes in olive oil

4 cloves minced garlic

1 large onion, sliced

1 jar artichokes in water

1 pkg chopped mushrooms

2 tbsp Italian seasoning

1 jar roasted red bell peppers

3 lbs. beef rump roast.

Directions:

Remove the fat, then slice into chunks. Place the meat into the Instant Pot with four cups of water.

Close and seal the lid. Set to manual for ten minutes. When done, quick release and remove the meat and place in a bowl. Get rid of the water and rinse the meat.

Place the meat back into the Instant Pot.

Julienne the bell peppers and rough chop artichokes. If the tomatoes are large, give them a rough chop, too.

Place all in the pot including the liquids from the jars of vegetables. Add sliced mushrooms, garlic, and Italian seasoning.

Close and seal the lid. Set to slow cook on high and cook for 20 minutes.

When done, naturally release pressure. Open the lid and remove the meat.

You can serve with Brussels sprouts or asparagus. Feel free to spoon the liquid in the pot over the meat to keep it moist and to season veggies.

Nutrition Information per Serving:

Calories: 246 Protein: 32g Carbohydrates: 8g net Fat: 12g

42. Carnitas

Serves: 12

Prep: 8 hours

Ingredients:

Water

2 limes, cut into wedges

2 grated carrots

1 head lettuce, washed and dried

2 tbsp olive oil

4 lbs. pork roast

Spice Mix:

1 tsp white pepper

1 large chopped onion

1 tsp cumin

1 tsp garlic powder

1 tbsp unsweetened cocoa powder

1 tsp salt

1/8 tsp coriander

1/8 tsp cayenne pepper

1 tsp red pepper flakes

2 tsp oregano

Directions:

Make the spice mix by mixing all of the spice mix ingredients together the day before. Cut the roast into manageable pieces and rub them with the spices. Place them and the onion in a zipper seal bag and refrigerate overnight.

Set the cooker to sauté and pour the olive oil. When hot, brown the roast pieces on all sides, then add enough water just covering the roast.

Close and seal the lid. Set on high and cook for 50 minutes. Turn off the pot and naturally release pressure. This will take about 20 minutes.

Open the lid and take out the meat. Shred the meat with forks.

Set the Instant Pot to sauté and allow the liquid to boil. Continue to boil until reduced. Strain and defat. The easiest way to defat is to leave in refrigerator overnight and take the fat solid on top off with spoon.

You can either put pork in the fridge or continue with instructions.

Place pork into the sauté pan and fry until browned. For added flavor put some cooking liquid on the pork before serving.

To assemble lettuce wraps: Fill the lettuce cups with carrots and fried pork. Finish with a squirt of lime juice.

Nutrition Information per Serving:

Calories: 450 Protein: 37g Carbohydrates: 5g net Fat: 31g

43. Chicken Cacciatore

Serves: 8

Prep: 10 minutes

Ingredients:

Pepper

1 green bell pepper, seeded and diced

Salt

Fresh parsley

1 can black olives

2 tbsp tomato paste

2 cans crushed tomatoes

6 boneless skinless chicken breasts

½ c chicken broth

8 oz sliced mushrooms

4 cloves crushed garlic

3 chopped shallots

Olive oil

Directions:

Set the cooker to sauté and pour some oil. When the oil is hot, add the bell pepper and shallots and cook for two minutes. Pour the broth and let it come to boil. Boil for three minutes and scrape all the good browned bits off bottom.

Add the garlic and mushrooms. Put on top of the chicken. Add crushed tomatoes on top. DO NOT STIR. Put tomato paste on top.

Close and seal the lid then set on high pressure. Cook for eight minutes then turn off the heat and let the pressure release. Take off the lid, add the pepper, salt, red pepper flakes, parsley, and olives.

Serve and enjoy.

Nutrition Information per Serving:

Calories: 234 Protein: 40g Carbohydrates: 7g net Fat: 6g

44. Tandoori Pork Ribs

Serves: 6

Prep: 5 minutes

Ingredients:

1 ½ tsp salt

3 cups water

4 tbsp Tandoori Spice

5 cloves garlic

½ c favorite barbecue sauce

1-inch ginger, roughly chopped

2 bay leaves

2 lbs. baby back ribs

Directions:

Slice the ribs so they will fit into the Instant Pot. Place in the pot as flat as possible. Stack if you need them. Add two tablespoons of spice mix, salt, garlic, ginger, and bay leaves.

Pour enough water to cover the meat.

Close and seal the lid. Set on high and cook for 22 minutes.

When finished, naturally release the pressure. Gently remove ribs and set on a plate. Place foil and cool for five minutes.

Pat dry and cover with barbecue sauce or more Tandoori spice.

Grill or broil for five minutes each side.

Serve.

Nutrition Information per Serving:

Calories: 160 Protein: 25g Carbohydrates: 4g net Fat: 4g

45.Mexican Beef

Serves: 6

Prep: 10 minutes

Ingredients:

Pepper

½ tsp fish sauce

1 tbsp tomato paste

2 ½ lbs. boneless beef chuck roast, diced

1 tbsp butter

6 cloves garlic

½ c broth

1 medium onion, thinly sliced

½ c salsa

1 tbsp chili powder

1 ½ tsp salt

Directions:

Combine the beef, salt, and chili powder. Set the Instant Pot to sauté. Add the butter and melt. Place the onions until soft.

Add the garlic and tomato sauce and give it a good stir. Add the beef. Pour fish sauce, stock, and salsa.

Cover and seal the lid. Set on meat and cook for 35 minutes.

When finished, naturally release the pressure. Take off the lid and season with pepper and salt.

Serve and enjoy.

Nutrition Information per Serving:

Calories: 500 Protein: 45g Carbohydrates: 8g net Fat: 9g

46. Saag

Serves: 6

Prep: 10 minutes

Ingredients:

2 medium diced onions

½ tsp black pepper

1 tsp cumin

1 tsp garam masala

2 tsp salt

2-inch piece ginger, minced

1 lb. mustard greens

½ tsp cayenne

4 cloves minced garlic

½ tsp turmeric

2 tbsp ghee

1 tsp coriander

1 lb. spinach

Directions:

Set the cooker to sauté and melt the ghee. Add the garlic, ginger, spices, and onion, then cook for three minutes. Add spinach and stir until begins to wilt then add the mustard greens.

Close and seal the lid. Set on poultry and cook for 15 minutes, then naturally release the pressure.

Using an immersion blender, puree to desired consistency.

Serve with some ghee on top.

Nutrition Information per Serving:

Calories: 150 Protein: 7.2g Carbohydrates: 8g net Fat: 8.7g

47.Coconut Lemongrass Chicken

Serves: 6

Prep: 10 minutes

Ingredients:

Pepper

Salt

1 large sliced onion

1 tsp five spice powder

3 tbsp coconut aminos

2 tbsp fish sauce

¼ c chopped scallions

1 c coconut milk

2-inch piece ginger

4 cloves minced garlic

Stalk lemongrass

10 drumsticks, skinless

Directions:

Put drumsticks in a bowl and season with pepper and salt.

Put lemongrass, five spice powder, coconut aminos, fish sauce, coconut milk, ginger, and garlic in your blender and mix everything together until there are no lumps.

Pour onto the chicken and toss to coat.

Put the onion in the bottom of the Instant Pot and place the drumsticks and sauce on top.

Close and seal the lid. Set to slow cook on low for four hours.

Nutrition Information per Serving:

Calories: 300 Protein: 18g Carbohydrates: 29g net Fat: 4g

48. Thai Chicken Broth

Serves: 10

Prep: 5 minutes

Ingredients:

5 slices ginger

20 fresh basil leaves

1 tbsp salt

1 stalk lemongrass, cut into chunks

1 whole chicken

1 lime

Directions:

Put salt, ginger, basil leaves, lemongrass, and chicken into the Instant Pot. Fill with water.

Set on slow cook for eight hours.

Ladle broth into a bowl then add salt to taste. Squeeze some lime juice and garnish with basil

Nutrition Information per Serving:

Calories: 290 Protein: 23g Carbohydrates: 17g net Fat: 6g

49.Jerk Chicken

Serves: 4 to 6

Prep: 8 minutes

Ingredients:

2 tsp garlic powder

1 tsp cayenne pepper

4 tsp paprika

1 tsp pepper

4 tsp salt

2 tsp thyme

2 tsp white pepper

2 tsp onion powder

5 chicken breasts

Directions:

Mix all the spices in a bowl. Rub each breast with spice mixture and place in the Instant Pot.

Close and seal the lid. Set on slow cook for six hours. Serve alongside your favorite keto side.

Nutrition Information per Serving:

Calories: 150 Protein: 26g Carbohydrates: 0g net Fat: 4g

50. Asian Beef Pot Roast

Serves: 12

Prep: 5 minutes

Ingredients:

2 tbsp sugar substitute

1 tsp red wine vinegar

1 tbsp orange zest

½ c water

1 tsp crushed red pepper flakes

¼ c fish sauce

1 tsp orange extract

2 tbsp fresh ginger, chopped

1 tbsp sugar substitute

3 garlic cloves, crushed

4 lb chuck roast

Sriracha sauce:

½ tsp orange zest

1 tsp sugar substitute

1 tsp sriracha sauce

¼ c mayonnaise

Directions:

Stir together the water, red pepper flakes, sweetener, fish sauce, orange extract, ginger, and garlic together. Rub this mixture over the chuck roast and place it into your Instant Pot.

Place the lid and lock it into place. Set to manual on high pressure for 35 minutes.

Once it's done, quick release the pressure and remove the lid.

Mix the red wine vinegar, orange zest, and a tablespoon of sweetener.

Shred up the meat and serve with your garnishes of choice.

As everything is cooking, stir together the orange sauce. Serve the roast with this mixture.

Nutrition Information per Serving:

Calories: 245 Protein: 9g Carbohydrates: 0g net Fat: 38g

51.Green Chili with Chicken

Serves: 4-6

Prep: 10 minutes

Ingredients:

6 garlic cloves, peeled

1 tbsp Asian fish sauce

½ c cilantro leaves

1 tbsp whole cumin seed, ground

1 medium onion chopped

6 oz Anaheim peppers, chopped

1 lb poblano peppers, chopped

Salt

¾ lb tomatillos, husks removed and quartered

2 serrano chilies, chopped

3 lb chicken thighs, bone-in, skin on

Directions:

Mix the cumin, garlic, onion, Serrano, Anaheim, poblano, tomatillos, and chicken in your Instant Pot and mix with a big pinch of salt. Close and lock the lid.

Set on high for 15 minutes, then release the pressure once it is done.

Take the chicken out with tongs and set aside. Stir the fish sauce and cilantro into the Instant Pot. Use a hand blender and puree the mixture. Add salt if need.

Remove the bones and skin from chicken and shred. Mix the chicken back into the mixture. Garnish with some extra cilantro and enjoy.

Nutrition Information per Serving:

Calories: 279.4 Protein: 42.1g Carbohydrates: 9.1g net Fat: 9.1g

52. Mexican Carnitas

Serves: 11 cups

Prep: 5 minutes

Ingredients:

½ tsp garlic powder

¼ tsp dry adobo seasoning

2 bay leaves

2-3 chipotle peppers in adobo

¾ c chicken broth

¼ tsp oregano

½ tsp sazon

1 ½ tsp cumin

6 garlic cloves

Pepper

2 tsp kosher salt

2 ½ lb pork shoulder, trimmed

Directions:

Sprinkle some pepper and salt over the pork. Heat a skillet and brown the pork on all sides. Set off the heat and let it cool.

Slice one-inch deep holes into the meat and insert a garlic sliver. Do this until you use up all of the garlic pieces. Sprinkle the garlic powder, adobo, oregano, Sazon, and cumin all over the pork.

Place the chicken broth in your Instant Pot and add the chipotle peppers and bay leaves. Set the pork into the Instant

Pot and place the lid, locking it into place. Set to the meat setting for 50 minutes.

Once done, release the pressure and shred the pork and mix with the juices. Take out the bay leaves and adjust any flavors that you need to.

Nutrition Information per Serving:

Calories: 190 Protein: 27g Carbohydrates: 1g net Fat: 8g

53. Corned Beef and Cabbage

Serves: 12 cups

Prep: 15 minutes

Ingredients:

2 tsp dried mustard

1 c carrots, sliced in thirds

4 garlic cloves

1 c onions, sliced

1 c celery, chopped

1 head cabbage, cut into wedges

2 tsp peppercorns

6 c water

4 lb corned beef brisket

Directions:

Put your beef brisket into your Instant Pot, and get rid of the spice pack that came with it.

Add water just enough to cover the brisket, then sprinkle the spices into the pot.

Place the lid and lock into place. Set the pot to meat/stew and set on high for 60 minutes.

Once it is done cooking, select cancel and let natural release happen for 20 minutes. Carefully take the lid off.

Take the brisket out and keep it warm. add the vegetables and place the lid back on. Set to soup for 15 minutes. Once done, quick release the pressure.

Place the beef back in and allow it to warm.

Serve and enjoy.

Nutrition Information per Serving:

Calories: 334 Protein: 23.7g Carbohydrates: 5.5g net Fat: 22.8g

54. Belizean Stewed Chicken

Serves: 8

Prep: 75 minutes

Ingredients:

1 tbsp sugar substitute

½ tsp pepper

2 tbsp recado rojo

2 tbsp white vinegar

2 c chicken stock

1 tsp oregano

3 sliced garlic cloves

3 tbsp Worcestershire sauce

1 tsp cumin

1 c onions, sliced

1 tbsp coconut oil

4 chicken drumsticks

4 chicken thighs

Directions:

Mix the sweetener, pepper, oregano, cumin, Worcestershire sauce, vinegar, and recado together. Rub marinade on chicken. Let sit for an hour.

Set the cooker to sauté and place the coconut oil. Place the chicken in and brown in batches. Take the chicken out and set aside.

Place the onion and garlic and allow them to sauté for a couple of minutes until they are soft.

Put the chicken back in. Add the chicken broth to the bowl that has the remaining marinade and mix together.

Pour this mixture over the chicken. Place the lid and seal into place.

Set on high for 20 minutes.

Once done, quick release the pressure, and adjust flavors if you need to.

Nutrition Information per Serving:

Calories: 410 Protein: 30g Carbohydrates: 6g net Fat: 24g

Vegetables

55.Spaghetti Squash

Serves: 2

Prep: 5 minutes

Ingredients:

1 c water

1 medium spaghetti squash

Directions:

Use a knife and slice the squash half crosswise. You get longer strands when the squash is cut crosswise instead of lengthwise.

Scoop all of the gunk and seeds out of the center of each squash half.

Set the trivet or steamer into your Instant Pot and pour the water.

Set the squash inside. You can place it in cut side up or cut side down; it doesn't matter.

Set the lid and lock it into place. Place the pot on manual on high heat for seven minutes.

Once the squash has cooked through, quick release the pressure and take off the lid.

If you cooked it with the cut side up, tip them over to remove the water from the center. Poke a fork into the squash to make sure it is tender.

Remove the squash and then pull the insides out.

Nutrition Information per Serving:

Calories: 31 Protein: 1g Carbohydrates: 7g net Fat: 1g

56. Mashed Cauliflower

Serves: 4

Prep: 1 minutes

Ingredients:

Handful chives

1 large head cauliflower, cut into chunks

1/8 tsp salt

1 c water

¼ tsp garlic powder

1 tbsp butter

1/8 tsp pepper

Directions:

Core the cauliflower and then dice it into large chunks.

Set the steamer basket or trivet into the bottom of the pot and add the water. Add the cauliflower on the trivet.

Place the lid and seal it into place.

Set to the manual setting in high pressure and let cook for three to five minutes.

Use the quick release so that the cauliflower doesn't become mush. Remove the lid.

Take out the inner pot and drain out the water.

Place the cauliflower into the pot once you have rinsed out.

Add all of the seasoning and the butter and mash them all together until it reaches the consistency that you like.

Nutrition Information per Serving:

Calories: 95 Protein: 2.9g Carbohydrates: 3g net Fat: 8g

57. Steamed Artichokes

Serves: 2-4

Prep: 5 minutes

Ingredients:

2 medium whole artichokes

1 c water

1 lemon wedge

Directions:

Rinse off your artichokes and get rid of any damaged outer leaves. Trim off the top third and the stem of the artichokes. Rub the lemon wedge across the top of the artichoke so that it doesn't brown.

Place the steamer rack into your Instant Pot and in the water. Set the artichokes on the steamer rack and lock the lid into place.

Place on manual mode and set the time for 20 minutes. If your artichokes are larger or smaller, adjust the time up or down by five minutes.

Once the cooking is done, turn off the machine, wait ten minutes, and then quick release the pressure. With tongs, carefully take out the artichokes and serve them with your dipping of choice.

Nutrition Information per Serving:

Calories: 60 Protein: 4.2g Carbohydrates: 6g net Fat: .2g

58. Brussel Sprouts

Serves: 4

Prep: 5 minutes

Ingredients:

1 tbsp honey

½ c water

Habanero sea salt

3-4 slices of bacon, chopped

4 c Brussel sprouts, chopped

Directions:

Cook the bacon in your pot on the sauté mode, making sure not to let them burn. Add the sprouts and allow them to cook for another five minutes.

Pour the water. Place the lid and lock into place. Set to manual on high for two minutes.

Release the pressure then take out the sprouts and sprinkle with a bit of salt.

Nutrition Information per Serving:

Calories: 56 Protein: 4g Carbohydrates: 7g net Fat: .8g

59. Turmeric Cauliflower Mash

Serves: 4

Prep: 1 minutes

Ingredients:

1 tbsp butter

3 chives, chopped

½ tsp pepper

1 ½ c water

½ tsp turmeric

1 head cauliflower

¼ tsp salt

Directions:

Place water in the pot. Put the steamer basket and add the cauliflower. Lock the lid and set to high for six minutes. Quick release the pressure.

Put the cauliflower in a bowl and mash. Mix the all the other ingredients, except the chives. Once mixed, garnish with fresh chives.

Nutrition Information per Serving:

Calories: 80 Protein: 4g Carbohydrates: 2g net Fat: 5g

60. Spaghetti Squash with Crispy Garlic Sauce

Serves: 4

Prep: 5 minutes

Ingredients:

1 medium spaghetti squash

1 tsp salt

1 small bunch sage

2 tbsp olive oil

1/8 tsp nutmeg

1 cup water

4 cloves garlic

Directions:

Halve the squash and remove the seeds.

Add water to the Instant Pot. Place squash halves in facing up. Stacking on top of each other is fine.

Close and seal the lid. Set on high and cook four minutes.

While cooking in cold sauté pan, put olive oil, garlic, and sage. Cook on low to fry sage leaves. The leaves will be dark green when crispy. Watch the garlic so it doesn't burn.

When timer goes off, quick release the pressure.

Using forks, shred spaghetti into the sauté pan. When all of the squash is in the pan, turn off the heat and sprinkle with nutmeg and salt. Stir everything to coat.

Serve with some Parmesan.

Nutrition Information per Serving:

Calories: 88.6 Protein: 1.5g Carbohydrates: 3g net Fat: 4g

61. Steamed Artichokes

Serves: 4

Prep: 5 minutes

Ingredients:

Pinch paprika

1 tsp Dijon mustard

1 lemon, sliced in half

2 tbsp mayonnaise

2 medium artichokes

Directions:

Wash the artichokes well and remove any damaged leaves. If they are spiny, cut off the top and trim the spines with kitchen shears.

Wipe the cut edges with lemon. This keeps them from turning brown.

If the artichoke came with a stem, slice it off to make a flat bottom. Peel and slice the stem and boil it in the water under the artichoke.

Add a cup of water to the Instant Pot. And put the steamer basket in. Put artichokes facing up and spritz with remaining lemon on top. Close and seal the lid. Set on high and cook for ten minutes.

When timer goes off, naturally release the pressure for ten minutes. Quick release the remaining pressure.

Check for doneness by removing an outer edge and give it a taste. If the leaf comes off easily, it's done. If not, cook for few more minutes.

Mix the mustard and mayonnaise and put into a dipping container. Sprinkle with paprika. Serve and enjoy.

Nutrition Information per Serving:

Calories: 77.5 Protein: 2g Carbohydrates: 3.5g net Fat: 5g

62. Prosciutto-wrapped Asparagus

Serves: 6

Prep: 5 minutes

Ingredients:

1 lb. asparagus

8 oz. thinly slice Prosciutto

Directions:

Put one cup water into the Instant Pot.

Wrap each asparagus spear with prosciutto. Put any unwrapped spears in single layer in bottom of the steamer basket. Lay the prosciutto wrapped asparagus on top in single layer. Put basket in the pot.

Close and seal the lid. Set the pot on high for three minutes. Once done, naturally release the pressure. Take out the steamer basket and put asparagus on serving platter.

Serve and enjoy.

Nutrition Information per Serving:

Calories: 39 Protein: 3g Carbohydrates: 2g net Fat: 2g

63. Cauli-Rice

Serves: 4

Prep: 5 minutes

Ingredients:

Lime wedge

Cilantro

¼ tsp paprika

¼ tsp turmeric

¼ tsp cumin

½ tsp parsley

¼ tsp salt

2 tbsp olive oil

Head of cauliflower

Directions:

Add a cup of water and steamer basket to the pot and add cauliflower. Lock the lid and set to manual for one minute. Once done, quick release the pressure.

Set cauliflower on a plate and get rid of the water in the pot. Set pot to sauté and add the oil and cauliflower.

Break it up with a masher and mix with the desired spices. Enjoy!

Nutrition Information per Serving:

Calories: 80 Protein: 1g Carbohydrates: 3g net Fat: 5g

64. Acorn Squash

Serves: 4

Prep: 2 minutes

Ingredients:

2 acorn squashes

½ c water

½ tsp salt

Directions:

Cut the squash in half, then remove the seeds. Put steamer basket in the Instant Pot with ½ cup water.

Put squash in the pot and sprinkle with salt.

Close and seal the lid and set on manual on high for five minutes. Quick release when done. Use fork to separate squash from peel.

Nutrition Information per Serving:

Calories: 114.8 Protein: 2.3g Carbohydrates: 20g net Fat: .3g

65. Butternut Squash

Serves: 4

Prep: 5 minutes

Ingredients:

¾ c water

1 tsp garlic powder

1 tbsp pumpkin pie spice

1 tbsp dried oregano

1 medium chopped onion

1 tsp chili powder

2 lb. chopped butternut squash

Directions:

Place all the ingredients into the Instant Pot, then stir to combine. ·

Close and seal the lid and set the pot on high for three minutes. Quick release the pressure once done. Enjoy!

Nutrition Information per Serving:

Calories: 102 Protein: 2.3g Carbohydrates: 21.5g net Fat: .2g

66. Kale and Carrots

Serves: 2

Prep: 10 minutes

Ingredients:

Balsamic vinegar

Pepper

1 medium onion, sliced

Salt

½ c chicken broth

5 cloves garlic, rough chopped

3 medium carrots, cut into ½-inch slices

1 tbsp ghee

10 oz. kale, rough chop

Directions:

Set the Instant Pot to sauté and melt the ghee. Add onions and carrots and cook until fragrant. Place the garlic and add the kale, then add the chicken broth and sprinkle with pepper and salt.

Close and seal the lid and set on manual on high and cook five minutes. When done, naturally release pressure, then take off the lid. Stir well to combine and splash some balsamic vinegar and whatever you would like to top it with.

Serve and enjoy.

Nutrition Information per Serving:

Calories: 150 Protein: 2g Carbohydrates: 5g net Fat: 0g

67.Summer Vegetable Soup

Serves: 6

Prep: 10 minutes

Ingredients:

Salt

Pepper

1 medium zucchini, sliced

1 small red bell pepper, chopped

½ c fresh basil

1 small orange bell pepper, chopped

½ c green beans

1 medium summer squash, sliced

1 medium onion, quartered

2 large tomatoes, seeded and sliced

1 small eggplant, sliced

6 cloves garlic

2 quarts broth

Directions:

Put all the ingredients into the Instant Pot, then close and seal the lid. Set the cooker to soup and cook for ten minutes. Once the timer beeps, naturally release the pressure. When done, remove the lid and using an immersion blender, puree the soup until smooth then add pepper and salt to taste.

Nutrition Information per Serving:

Calories: 102 Protein: 4.5g Carbohydrates: 11.8g net Fat: 2.6g

68.Spring Vegetable Soup

Serves: 6

Prep: 10 minutes

Ingredients:

Salt

Pepper

1 bunch asparagus, tough ends discarded

1 bunch radishes, about ten

5 small carrots, tops removed

1 medium leek

½ lb. spring greens like baby spinach

1 head garlic, peeled

1 onion, peeled and quartered

2 quarts broth

Directions:

Put all the ingredients except pepper and salt into the Instant Pot. Close and seal the lid.

Set the cooker on soup and cook for ten minutes. When finished, quick release the pressure and take off the lid. Puree soup with immersion blender then add pepper and salt to taste.

Serve and enjoy.

Nutrition Information per Serving:

Calories: 45 Protein: 2g Carbohydrates: 8g net Fat: 1g

69. Cauli-Rice

Serves: 4

Prep: 5 minutes

Ingredients:

Lime wedges

2 tbsp olive oil

Cilantro

¼ tsp cumin

¼ tsp turmeric

¼ tsp paprika

½ tsp dried parsley

¼ tsp salt

1 medium or large head cauliflower

Directions:

Wash cauliflower and remove any leaves. Chop into large pieces. Put into steamer basket of the Instant Pot.

Pour one cup of water into the bottom of the Instant Pot. Place steamer basket inside. Close and seal the lid.

Set on manual on high for one minute. When timer beeps, quick release the pressure. Put cauliflower on a plate, then remove the water from the Instant Pot.

Put pot back into the Instant Pot. Set on sauté. Add oil and cauliflower. Mash with a potato masher. You can add any other spices or seasonings at this point. Taste and adjust salt if needed.

Nutrition Information per Serving:

Calories: 20 Protein: 2g Carbohydrates: 2g net Fat: 0g

70. Beet Borscht

Serves: 6

Prep: 15 minutes

Ingredients:

1 tbsp salt

Bay leaf

3 large peeled beets

6 cups stock

3 c shredded cabbage

½ tbsp. thyme

1 medium diced onion

¼ c dill

2 cloves diced garlic

2 large carrots diced

½ c sour cream

3 stalks celery diced

Directions:

Put washed beets in the steamer basket of the Instant Pot with one cup of water. Steam for seven minutes, then quick release the pressure and drop the beets into an ice bath. Skins should come right off. Dice the beets. If you don't want your hands red, wear gloves.

Add the thyme, salt, stock, bay leaf, cabbage, onions, garlic, celery, carrots, and beets to the Instant Pot.

Set on soup and cook for 45 minutes.

Once done, naturally release pressure. Serve and enjoy.

Nutrition Information per Serving:

Calories: 163 Protein: 12g Carbohydrates: 20g net Fat: 2.5g

71. Onion Soup

Serves: 4

Prep: 10 minutes

Ingredients:

1 tbsp balsamic vinegar

2 sprigs thyme

1 tsp salt

6 cups stock

2 bay leaves

8 cups onions, sliced into half moons

2 tbsp coconut oil

Directions:

Set the cooker to sauté and pour the oil. When oil is heated, add onions and sauté until translucent.

Pour in balsamic and deglaze. Add thyme, bay leaves, salt, and stock. Close and seal the lid then set on high and cook for ten minutes. Once done, naturally release the pressure. Throw away the thyme stems and bay leaves. Blend the soup with an immersion blender.

Nutrition Information per Serving:

Calories: 113.2 Protein: 7.5g Carbohydrates: 14.7g net Fat: 3.5g

72. Brussels Sprouts

Serves: 6

Prep: 10 minutes

Ingredients:

Olive oil

Salt

Pepper

1 pomegranate

¼ c pine nuts, toasted

1 lb. Brussels sprouts

Directions:

Remove the outer leaves and trim stems from Brussels sprouts. Cut the larger ones in half. Add one cup of water to the Instant Pot and the steamer basket. Put the sprouts into the basket. Close and seal the lid and set on high. When pot reaches pressure, cook for three minutes, then quick release the pressure. Place on a serving dish and drizzle with olive oil, pine nuts, pomegranate seeds, pepper, and salt.

Nutrition Information per Serving:

Calories: 75 Protein: 5.4g Carbohydrates: 9.4g net Fat: .2g

Specialty

73.Buffalo Ranch Chicken Dip

Serves: 8

Prep: 2 minutes

Ingredients:

1 packet ranch dip mix

8 oz cream cheese

16 oz cheddar cheese

1 stick butter

1 lb chicken breast

1 c hot sauce

Directions:

Put the ranch dip packet, hot sauce, butter, cream cheese, and chicken inside of your Instant Pot.

Place the lid and lock it into place and then set it on high for 15 minutes.

Once done, release the pressure.

Take off the lid and shred up the chicken with a fork.

Mix the cheddar cheese and serve with your favorite keto friendly chips or veggies.

Nutrition Information per Serving:

Calories: 490 Protein: 30.6g Carbohydrates: 2.5g net Fat: 40.2g

74. Hard Boiled Eggs

Serves: 16

Prep: 1 minutes

Ingredients:

1 c water

16 eggs

Directions:

Set your wire rack into the bottom of your Instant Pot and add the water.

Set the eggs on the rack and make sure that are tight together. 16 eggs are normally how many eggs you can fit in it in a single layer, but it will depend on the size of the egg that you use. Place the lid and lock it into place. Select the manual button and set the time to four minutes on high pressure. Once it is done, quick release the pressure. Make sure you remove them quickly because they will overcook.

Carefully remove the eggs using a serving spoon and place in cold water for five minutes. Peel the eggs and enjoy.

Nutrition Information per Serving:

Calories: 70 Protein: 6g Carbohydrates: .9g net Fat: 4.5g

75. Crustless Cheesecake

Serves: 8

Prep: 5 minutes

Ingredients:

2 eggs, room temp

Handful strawberries

2 8 oz softened cream cheese

2/3 c favorite sugar substitute

1 tsp vanilla

Directions:

Take a springform pan and grease the inside well.

Using a mixer, beat the cream cheese until smooth and they don't have any lumps.

Mix the vanilla and sugar until it is all well incorporated.

Mix the eggs. Continue to beat together until they come together completely. Make sure not to over mix.

Pour this into your prepared springform pan. Place foil around the bottom and sides of the pan so that water doesn't leak into the pan.

Set a rack into the bottom of your Instant Pot. Pour enough water into your pot and ease the springform pan and set on the rack.

Place the lid and lock into place. Cook on high for 20 minutes.

Allow all of the pressure to release naturally, and let the cheesecake cool for 15 to 20 minutes in the Instant Pot.

Carefully ease the cheesecake out and allow it to come down to room temperature. Carefully take the foil off the bottom of the pan.

Place on saran wrap and refrigerate for a few hours. Before you serve, dice some strawberries and spread them on top.

Nutrition Information per Serving:

Calories: 213.5 Protein: 5.8g Carbohydrates: 4.9g net Fat: 20.8g

76. Cheesecake

Serves: 8

Prep: 10 minutes

Ingredients:

Filling:

¼ c heavy whipping cream

3 room temperature eggs

Zest of 1 lemon

1 tsp orange zest

½ tsp vanilla

½ c + 2 tbsp granulated swerve

16 oz. cream cheese, room temperature

Top Layer

2 tsp granulated swerve

½ c sour cream

Directions:

Use a 6-inch spring form pan. Take some parchment paper that is a bit larger than the pan and line the perimeter of the pan. Lightly oil the bottom of the pan. Wrap foil around the bottom.

Using hand held mixer, blend vanilla, orange zest, lemon zest, cream cheese, swerve, and heavy cream until smooth. Add the eggs until smooth.

Pour into the prepared pan. Lay a paper towel on top and wrap foil over top to hold towel in place. Set aside.

Pour one and a half cups water into the pot. Place trivet in water with handles up. Make a sling out of tin foil. Put the cheesecake in center of sling and carefully place it in the Instant Pot. Leave the sling in place.

Close the lid and seal. Press manual and set time for 37 minutes. While cheesecake cooks, fix the topping. Add topping ingredients to bowl and mix well to combine.

When the timer goes off, allow the pressure to release naturally for 18 minutes. Open valve and take off the lid.

Carefully lift the cheesecake out of the Instant Pot. Take off the foil and paper towel from the top. If there is liquid on cheesecake carefully blot it off. While cheesecake is hot, spread on the toppings.

Put the towel and foil on cheesecake and put in the refrigerator overnight. Once cooled, release the outer spring of pan and remove. Carefully take off the parchment paper. Cut into eight equal slices and serve.

Nutrition Information per Serving:

Calories: 268.1 Protein: 6.8g Carbohydrates: 3g net Fat: 23.8g

77. Chocolate Cake

Serves: 10

Prep: 10 minutes

Ingredients:

tsp vanilla

¾ c heavy cream

2 tsp baking powder

4 large eggs

½ c unsalted butter, melted

¼ tsp salt

¼ c chocolate protein powder

2/3 c unsweetened cocoa powder

¾ c swerve sweetener

1 ½ c almond flour

Directions:

Grease the Instant Pot. Mix salt, baking powder, protein powder, cocoa powder, sweetener, and almond flour together.

Add the vanilla extract, cream, eggs, and butter. Mix well to combine. Pour into the Instant Pot. Set to slow cook on low and cook for 3 hours.

Turn off and allow to cool for about 20 minutes. Serve.

Nutrition Information per Serving:

Calories: 344 Protein: 12.8g Carbohydrates: 6.5g net Fat: 29.3g

78. Breakfast Frittata

Serves: 6

Prep: 10 minutes

Ingredients:

½ tsp pepper

8 eggs

1 ½ c bell pepper, diced

¼ c diced red onion

1 tsp salt

1 1/3 c cooked breakfast sausage

¾ c frozen spinach, thawed and drained

Directions:

Combine the sausage, salt, pepper, eggs, red onions, bell pepper, spinach. Pour into the greased Instant Pot.

Set on slow cook on low for three hours until frittata is set.

Nutrition Information per Serving:

Calories: 238 Protein: 20g Carbohydrates: 3g net Fat: 16g

79. Sausage and Egg Casserole

Serves: 8

Prep: 10 minutes

Ingredients:

Pepper

Salt

2 cloves minced garlic

¾ c whipping cream

10 eggs

1 c shredded cheddar cheese

12 oz pkg. link sausage, cooked and sliced

1 medium broccoli head, chopped

Directions:

Grease the Instant Pot, then layer half of the broccoli, sausage, and cheese. Repeat the layer. Whisk eggs, pepper, salt, garlic, and whipping cream until combined. Pour over the ingredients. Close and seal the lid then place on slow cook for five hours. Edges should be browned and set in center.

Nutrition Information per Serving:

Calories: 484 Protein: 26.13g Carbohydrates: 4.21g net Fat: 38.6g

80. Granola

Serves: 12

Prep: 10 minutes

Ingredients:

½ c swerve

1 tsp salt

1 c pumpkin seeds

½ c raw almonds

½ c raw walnuts

1 tsp vanilla extract

½ c raw pecans

½ c raw hazelnuts

1 c raw sunflower seeds

1 tsp vanilla Stevia

1 tsp ground cinnamon

1 c unsweetened shredded coconut

1/3 c coconut oil

Directions:

Set the cooker to sauté then add the coconut oil and melt. When melted, add the vanilla extract and Stevia. Stir well before adding coconut, seeds, and nuts. Stir mixture well to coat all ingredients.

In bowl whisk salt, cinnamon, and swerve then sprinkle with seeds and nuts.

Close and seal the lid. Set on slow cook on low for two hours and stir every 30 minutes.

When done, quick release the pressure. Spread onto baking pan to cool and store in an airtight container.

Nutrition Information per Serving:

Calories: 337 Protein: 7.9g Carbohydrates: 4.8g net Fat: 31.6g

81. Buffalo Chicken Meatballs

Serves: 18-24 meatballs

Prep: 10 minutes

Ingredients:

Chopped green onions – garnish

2 garlic cloves, minced

4 tbsp butter

6 tbsp hot sauce

2 green onions, sliced

1 tsp sea salt

¾ c almond meal

1 ½ lb ground chicken

2 tbsp ghee

Directions:

Mix together the green onions, garlic, salt, almond meal, and chicken together. It helps to use your hands, and make sure you don't over mix it.

Use some ghee to grease your hands and start forming the meat into balls that are about two inches wide.

Place the Instant Pot on the sauté setting and place the ghee, allowing it to melt.

Work in batches, and place the meatballs into the pot to brown. Brown all sides for a minute.

While meatballs cook, mix together the butter and hot sauce and cook in the microwave until the butter is melted.

Once all the meatballs are browned, place them all in the pot and add the sauce on top

Lock the lid on, then set the pot to poultry.

Once the meatballs have finished cooking, quick release the pressure and enjoy.

Nutrition Information per Serving:

Calories: 290 Protein: 15g Carbohydrates: 5g net Fat: 11g

82. Meatballs

Serves: 5

Prep: 10 minutes

Ingredients:

1/3 c warm water

¼ tsp oregano

¼ tsp garlic powder

2 eggs

1 tsp olive oil

½ c almond flour

¾ c parmesan

1 tsp dried onion flakes

1 tsp kosher salt

2 tbsp parsley, chopped

1 ½ lb ground beef

¼ tsp pepper

3 c keto marinara sauce

Directions:

Stir everything together, minus the marinara sauce and olive oil. Mix well by hand and form the mixture into two-inch meatballs.

Add the olive oil to the pot.

Set the pot to sauté and brown all of the meatballs. Once all are browned, lay all the meatballs in the pot. Make sure you don't press them down.

Pour the marinara sauce and coat the meatballs.

Set on the lid and seal it into place. Set the pot to manual and set to low pressure for ten minutes.

Quick release the pressure once the cooking is done.

Take off the lid and serve with spaghetti squash or zoodles.

Nutrition Information per Serving:

Calories: 393 Protein: 30g Carbohydrates: 3g net Fat: 28g

83. Chicken Broth

Serves: 12 cups

Prep: 5 minutes

Ingredients:

3 to 4 liters water

2 garlic cloves

1 c chopped celery

2 tbsp apple cider vinegar

1 small onion, quartered – skin on

1-inch knob ginger

1 cooked chicken carcass, most meats removed

Directions:

Stir everything together and add water up to the four-liter mark. Place the lid and lock into place then set the cooker on high for 60 minutes.

After the time is up, quick release the pressure and allow the mixture to sit for an hour and cool.

Strain all of the solids out into a clean pot or container. Add some sea salt if you need to.

Allow it to chill for a while so that that the fat hardens on top.

Scrape any solid fat off. Portion the mixture into bowls and keep in the fridge for a week or freeze for three months.

Nutrition Information per Serving:

Calories: 10 Protein: 1g Carbohydrates: 1g net Fat: .5g

84. Boiled Peanuts

Serves: 4

Prep: 5 minutes

Ingredients:

1/3 c sea salt

Water

1 lb raw peanuts

Directions:

Go through the peanuts and get rid of debris and broken pieces. Rinse them off and place in your pot.

Place the salt and the fill with water until peanuts are covered. Stir everything together. Peanuts float, so set the trivet on top with a bowl to weight them down.

Place the lid and lock into place. Set to manual for 80 minutes then release the pressure and take out the nuts.

Nutrition Information per Serving:

Calories: 200 Protein: 8.5g Carbohydrates: 7g net Fat: 13.9g

85. Jalapeno Popper Dip

Serves: 8

Prep: 3 minutes

Ingredients:

½ c water

½ c almond flour

¾ c sour cream

8 oz cheddar cheese

3 sliced jalapenos

8 oz cream cheese

1 lb chicken breast

Directions:

Put the water, cream cheese, jalapenos, and chicken in your pot. Place the lid and lock, then set the cooker on high for 12 minutes.

Release pressure and shred chicken.

Mix six ounces of the cheddar cheese and the sour cream.

Put in a dish and the rest of the cheese and the almond flour. Place under a broiler for a couple of minutes and enjoy.

Nutrition Information per Serving:

Calories: 241 Protein: 5.2g Carbohydrates: 2.3g net Fat: 24.8g

86. Artichoke Dip

Serves: 8

Prep: 5 minutes

Ingredients:

3 garlic cloves

½ c mayo

½ c sour cream

14 oz can artichoke hearts

1 tsp onion powder

½ c chicken broth

8 oz shredded mozzarella

16 oz shredded parmesan

10 oz box frozen spinach

8 oz cream cheese

Directions:

Add a half cup of the chicken broth and three garlic cloves to the pot. Drain artichokes and mix. Mix the spinach, onion powder, mayo, cream cheese, and sour cream. Lock the lid and set the cooker to high for four minutes.

Quick release the pressure and mix the cheese. Place in a bowl and serve with your favorite dippers.

Nutrition Information per Serving:

Calories: 500 Protein: 7.4g Carbohydrates: 8g net Fat: 25g

87.Mini Chocolate Cakes

Serves: 2

Prep: 5 minutes

Ingredients:

2 tbsp heavy cream

¼ c baking cocoa

½ tsp baking powder

2 tbsp Splenda

1 tsp vanilla

2 eggs

Directions:

Stir everything together in a bowl. Grease two ramekins and split the batter between the two. Place a cup of water to the pot and set in the trivet.

Set the ramekins and lock the lid in place the set the cooker on high for nine minutes. Quick release the pressure and then flip the cakes onto a plate.

Nutrition Information per Serving:

Calories: 120 Protein: .8g Carbohydrates: 7g net Fat: 4.8g

88. Poached Eggs

Serves: 4-5

Prep: 5 minutes

Ingredients:

1 c water

4-5 eggs

Directions:

Set your trivet into the pot and add a cup of water.

Coat silicone cups with nonstick spray and crack an egg into each.

Set the cups into your pot. Lock the lid into place and set to steam and set to the time you need for your desired doneness.

Quick release the pressure and take off the lid. Lift out the cups and enjoy.

Nutrition Information per Serving:

Calories: 70 Protein: 6.3g Carbohydrates: .4g net Fat: 5g

89. Ricotta Lemon Cheesecake

Serves: 6

Prep: 5 minutes

Ingredients:

2 eggs

½ tsp lemon extract

1 lemon, juice and zest

1/3 c ricotta

¼ c truvia

8 oz cream cheese

Topping:

1 tsp truvia

2 tbsp sour cream

Directions:

Beat all the ingredients together except for the eggs until there are no lumps. Mix the eggs. Don't over beat. Pour this into a greased springform pan and place foil over the top.

Add two cups of water and the trivet in your pot and set on the cake. Lock the lid and set to high for 30 minutes. Let pressure release naturally.

Stir together the Truvia and sour cream. Spread this over the warm cake and refrigerate for six to eight hours.

Nutrition Information per Serving:

Calories: 190 Protein: 8g Carbohydrates: 6g net Fat: 9g

90. Wheat Belly Yogurt

Serves: 4

Prep: 5 minutes

Ingredients:

2 tbsp full-fat yogurt with live cultures

16 oz heavy whipping cream

Directions:

Stir the ingredients together in a glass bowl. Place in your Instant Pot and follow the yogurt making instructions.

Nutrition Information per Serving:

Calories: 149 Protein: 8.5g Carbohydrates: 7g net Fat: 8g

91. Raspberry Coffee Cake

Serves: 12

Prep: 15 minutes

Ingredients:

½ tsp vanilla

2/3 c water

3 eggs

1 ½ tsp baking powder

¼ c coconut flour

½ c swerve

6 tbsp butter, melted

1 ¼ c almond flour

¼ c protein powder

¼ tsp salt

Filling:

1 ½ c raspberries

2 tbsp whipping cream

1 egg

1/3 c swerve

8 oz cream cheese

Directions:

Grease the inside of your pot. Stir the dry ingredients together and then mix the water, butter, and eggs. Place to the side.

Beat the cream cheese and then mix the remaining ingredients, except raspberries. Place 2/3 of the first batter you made in your pot and smooth. Add cream cheese and spread across then add the raspberries. Dot the rest of the first batter on top.

Close the lid and set the cooker to slow cook for 3-4 hours. Enjoy

Nutrition Information per Serving:

Calories: 239 Protein: 7.54g Carbohydrates: 6.9g net Fat: 19g

92. Eggs in a Cup

Serves: 4

Prep: 5 minutes

Ingredients:

Pepper and salt

¼ c half & half

2 tbsp cilantro

½ c cheddar cheese

½ c shredded cheese

1 c diced veggies

4 eggs

Directions:

Combine the cilantro, pepper, salt, half & half, cheese, veggies, and eggs and divide into four-pint jars. Loosely place on lids.

Add two cups water to the pot and trivet. Set the jars. Lock the lid and set the cooker on high for five minutes. Once done, release the pressure.

Add other cheese and broil for a few minutes.

Nutrition Information per Serving:

Calories: 115 Protein: 9g Carbohydrates: 2g net Fat: 9g

93. Vanilla Bean Cheesecake

Serves: 8

Prep: 5 minutes

Ingredients:

Raspberry jam

1 vanilla bean, scraped

½ c swerve

1 tsp vanilla

2 eggs

16 oz cultured cream cheese

Directions:

Whisk everything together in a blender. Add to a springform pan and cover with foil. Add two cups of water to the pot and set on a rack.

Ease in the pan and lock the lid then set the cooker on high for 20 minutes. Once done, naturally release pressure. Take out of the pot and let it cool to room temp. Refrigerate at least an hour before serving.

Nutrition Information per Serving:

Calories: 100 Protein: 6g Carbohydrates: 8g net Fat: 10g

94. Greek Yogurt

Serves: 14

Prep: 5 minutes

Ingredients:

2 tbsp yogurt starter

1-gallon milk

Directions:

Place milk in the cooker. Cover lid and press the yogurt button and adjust to boil. Whisk every now and then during the cooking time.

Check the temperature once done, should be 180. If not, cook again. Once hot, take pot out and set in a cold water and whisk until it cools to 95-110.

Remove a bit of milk and mix the starter. Mix back in. Place back in the Instant Pot and place the lid and press yogurt, adjust to 8:00. Remove the pot and refrigerate until cold. Don't stir.

Strain milk through yogurt strainer for the Greek yogurt

Nutrition Information per Serving:

Calories: 220 Protein: 20g Carbohydrates: 9g net Fat: 11g

95. Garlic Spread

Serves: varies

Prep: 2 minutes

Ingredients:

Salt

2 tbsp olive oil

5-6 garlic heads

Directions:

Place 2/3 cup water in your pot and set in steamer basket. Cut the top off the garlic head. Set the garlic heads and drizzle with oil

Lock the lid then set the cooker to high pressure for ten minutes. Reduce the pressure and remove the garlic then sprinkle with salt. Once cool, remove cloves and mash together with a fork. Keep in the fridge.

Nutrition Information per Serving:

Calories: 34 Protein: 0g Carbohydrates: 5g net Fat: 2g

96.Peanut Butter Cheesecake

Serves: 8

Prep: 5 minutes

Ingredients:

1 tsp vanilla

1 tbsp cocoa

½ c swerve

2 tbsp powdered peanut butter

2 eggs

16 oz cream cheese

Directions:

Blend together eggs and cream cheese, and then add all the other ingredients. Place in four or eight-ounce jars and loosely place the lid.

Place a cup of water to the pot and set the trivet. Set the jars, lock the lid and set the cooker to high for 15-18 minutes. Once done, release pressure and remove.

Nutrition Information per Serving:

Calories: 191 Protein: 6g Carbohydrates: 5g net Fat: 16g

97. Dark Chocolate Cake

Serves: 10

Prep: 10 minutes

Ingredients:

½ c chocolate chips

¼ tsp salt

½ c cocoa powder

¾ tsp vanilla

6 tbsp butter, melted

1 ½ tsp baking powder

2/3 c almond milk

3 eggs

3 tbsp protein powder

½ c swerve

1 c + 2 tbsp almond flour

Directions:

Grease your pot and in a bowl, mix together the salt, baking powder, protein powder, cocoa powder, sweetener, almond flour. Mix the other ingredients into the dry ingredients and pour into your pot. Place the lid then set to slow cook for two and a half hours. Turn off and let it cool for 30 minutes. Serve.

Nutrition Information per Serving:

Calories: 220 Protein: 2g Carbohydrates: 8g net Fat: 4g

98. Breakfast Pie

Serves: 4-6

Prep: 10 minutes

Ingredients:

1 onion, diced

1 lb breakfast sausage

1 tbsp garlic powder

Pepper and salt

1 yam, shredded

8 eggs, whisked

2 tsp basil

Directions:

Grease your pot with oil. Place everything in your pot and mix all together. Place the lid and set to slow cook for 6-8 hours. Slice and enjoy.

Nutrition Information per Serving:

Calories: 220 Protein: 10g Carbohydrates: 6g net Fat: 8g

99.Pumpkin Pecan Cake

Serves: 10

Prep: 5 minutes

Ingredients:

¼ tsp salt

1 tsp ginger

¼ c protein powder

4 eggs

1 c pumpkin puree

¼ tsp cloves

1 tsp vanilla

1 ½ tsp cinnamon

¼ c butter, melted

2 tsp baking powder

1/3 c coconut flour

¾ c swerve

1 ½ c raw pecan

Directions:

Grease your pot, then grind pecans in a processor. Place in a bowl and mix the spices, sweetener, and coconut. Mix the vanilla, butter, eggs, and pumpkin. Spread into the pot. Place the lid and set to slow cook for 2 ½ hours. Enjoy.

Nutrition Information per Serving:

Calories: 250 Protein: 7g Carbohydrates: 8g net Fat: 17g

100. Brussels Sprout Dip

Serves: 4

Prep: 10 minutes

Ingredients:

1 lb brussels sprouts

¼ c sour cream

4 oz cream cheese

½ tsp thyme

¼ c mayo

¾ c mozzarella, shredded

2 garlic cloves

¼ c parmesan

1 tbsp olive oil

Directions:

Coat sprouts with oil, pepper, and salt. Bake the garlic and sprouts at 400 for 20-30 minutes. Flip half way.

Remove skins from garlic, then mix everything in your pot. Place the lid and set to slow cook for 2-4 hours.

Nutrition Information per Serving:

Calories: 250 Protein: 15g Carbohydrates: 2g net Fat: 16g

101. Chocolate Cake

Serves: 10

Prep: 5 minutes

Ingredients:

2/3 c cocoa powder, unsweetened

¾ c heavy cream

4 eggs

1 tsp vanilla

¼ c chocolate protein powder

½ c butter, melted

¼ tsp salt

2 tsp baking powder

¾ c swerve

1 ½ c almond flour

Directions:

Grease your pot well. Beat everything together until smooth then pour into the pot. Place the lid and set to slow cook for two and a half hours. Turn off and let cool for about 20-30 minutes. Serve warm.

Nutrition Information per Serving:

Calories: 325 Protein: 13g Carbohydrates: 6.5g net Fat: 12g

Conclusion

Thank for making it through to the end of *Ketogenic Diet Instant Pot*. Let's hope it was informative and able to provide you with all of the tools you need to achieve your goals.

The next step is to start trying out some of these recipes to make your keto lifestyle easier and more delicious.

Finally, if you found this book useful in any way, a review o will help me a lot and is always appreciated!

Keto
Meal Prep

The essential Ketogenic Meal prep guide for beginners (30 Days Meal Prep)

Written By

Alicia J. Taylor

INTRODUCTION

I would like to start off by expressing my utmost gratitude and appreciation to you and your kind gesture for purchasing my book. I have tried my very best to make sure that this extremely accessible to keto Meal Prep aficionados who like to learn Instructions lead a healthy lifestyle!

In doing so, I have divided the book into three parts. The first part of the book will help you to fully grasp the basic concepts of Meal Prepping, so if you are new to Meal Prepping, you will be able to master the techniques in no time, while the second part will teach you how you can build up your very own Meal Plan!

And finally, the Third part is the recipe galore, where I present you with a 30-day Meal Plan filled with delicious Ketogenic recipes that are healthy and heartwarming dishes that can be easily implemented to your Meal Prep plan with minimal effort.

I have tried my very best to keep the recipes short and as easy as possible to make! However, there might be some longer recipes, but those are particularly for individuals who like to experience a bit of "Challenge!" Don't be alarmed as there are plenty of recipes for beginners as well!

That being said, I welcome you to your amazing venture into the world of Keto Meal Prepping!

God Bless!

Chapter 1: Why Should I Meal Prep?

Everyone has a busy schedule and with busy timings and tough working hours, it is very difficult to prepare a good and healthy meal. Meal preparation is one way to control yourself from over eating and from eating excess carb diet. If you prepare meals ahead of time you can achieve the perfect diet goals.

Meal preparation comes in many forms and shapes. A typical meal preparation should include a preparation of meals for one single day or five days. A person can also prepare a meal for each day or else prepare it in in bulk to save up time. You could also cut vegetables and chop them before head to save up time for your meal preparations.

No matter how busy you are or whatever tough schedule you have preparing a healthy and balanced meal should be your first priority. Having said that, a healthy meal does not necessarily mean a meal with only leafy raw vegetables but one which is appealing to the eye and tongue both. A good meal is one which not only tastes well but is presented beautifully as well. Experts say that the first thing which they notice on the plate is what they see not what they eat.

Preparing your meal ahead of time can give you a lot of good time to think about what is your favorite meal and you can even set up your meals according to the portion sizes so that you do not over eat and gain weight.

If you have your food prepared at home, you will not have the urge to go out and eat as it will be in your mind already that you have a good meal already prepared for yourself. While you do the effort of preparing your meal, you have this excellent opportunity to select the ingredients according to your own wish and select your own favorite ingredients.

102. <u>Proper plan for meal preparation is required:</u>

With a proper plan about meal preparation in your mind you can prevent from making unnecessary purchases and you can avoid buying stuff which is not at all needed which will ultimately save time and prevent food from being wasted as well.

A good meal requires proper planning and proper meal preparation. If your meal is prepared ahead of time it can ease up your stress level and you do not have to be in a rush to prepare your meal on time or be worried about being late. Punctuality is the key to success when you want your meal to be ready on time.

Preparing your meals, yourself and at home is a complete win - win situation without any comparison. With the food ready on the table and having ample amount of time to plan what to cook for your meal can having many benefits.

Preparing meals at home saves up a lot of time and money both. Packaged foods may taste good and also more appealing to the eye rather than homemade foods but packaged foods might not be having the same nutritional value as compared to the homemade foods. Packaged foods might be presentable, but they will be costly for you and will not be able to beat the hygiene that you own homemade food possesses.

Going out of the home to have your lunch or dinner will take up a lot of time and waste it like anything. At home on the other hand, you neither need to place an order and wait for the peak hour to end or anything. You just need to get up and have your meal in peace without paying a hefty amount of cash.

The foods out there in the restaurants have high amounts of salts and carbs in them. Neither salt not carbs are good for your health which is why it is better to eat food at your home with balanced spices and salt added to it.

One of the best reasons of preparing your meal at home is that it is the perfect way to bring the family closer and gives a lot of time to understand each other and talk about themselves. You have the perfect option of getting closer to your family members and talk with them one on one.

103.   The importance of meal preparation:

It is extremely important to prepare your meal for health reasons and to stay fit. If you wish to succeed in your health and fitness goals, you need to prepare meals ahead of time. With your meal prepared ahead of time, you do not need to worry about going to a local café and eating food that does not have any nutrition and is full of calories as well.

When you feel hungry at home and your meal is already prepared you just need to dig in which will keep your metabolism humming. If the meal is not prepared, you need to first go out somewhere and search for food and wait until you get it. This can take a long time and your metabolic process might be disturbed as well.

Preparing a meal is important because it saves up your time and money both. You do not need to spend a heft amount just for a single serving and then regret it later. The food you get outside is much more expensive than the one you have at your home. You can compare the prices and the cost yourself and you will be amazed.

104. <u>**Simple meal preparation ideas:**</u>

It is not at all complicated to prepare a full-fledged meal for yourself and your family members. Here are a few tips for you to plan a simple meal at your home.

- Make dinner or lunch in a good quantity so that you can use it the next day as well and it will save up your time and energy both. You can use airtight plastic containers and even freeze your food. You just need to microwave the next day and there you go!
- If you are a salad lover, all you need to do is to chop some veggies and put them in a tray to roast in the oven and use your salad as a sideline.
- Chose simple foods such as protein balls, fresh and juicy fruits and almonds for snacks.
- Prepare soups in a good quantity and then freeze them for later use.
- Boil a few eggs for the whole week and then keep eating them the whole week so your lunch is healthy and full of nutrition.
- Use a griller to grill your chicken or meat and then freeze them for later use.
- Buy salad mixes from the supermarket but make sure that they do not have lots of carbs in them or loads of sugar. You can then use these mixes to drizzle over your salad and they will be delicious to eat.
- With the help of a big pan, cook lots of brown rice or quinoa so that you can eat it cold during the whole week.

105. Eat more, weigh less?

Have you ever tried to lose weight by cutting down on food? Do you feel hungry after eating less food than you normally do? Does it make you angry not being satisfied with the amount of food you eat?

There are other ways of weighing less that is a more steady and slow approach towards aiming for weight loss. You can do this by cutting down calories in your diet, taking a nutritional diet and perform good physical activity. With this kind of diet plan, you will not only be satisfied, but you will also be healthy.

A research conducted revealed that people lose weight by cutting down on the number of calories, not by cutting the serving of the food. You could do this by lowering the calorie intake and eat foods that have less calories and increase fiber foods in your diet. Foods that are rich in fiber content are not only healthy but they will contribute greatly towards weight loss.

The average calorie intake that a person should take is 1200 calories per day. An example is a plate of mac and cheese. By the looks and sound of it, we feel that it is a super cheesy meal and it has 540 calories in one plate that serves 1.

You could remake this plate and serve it with fewer calories and still it will taste delicious. For example, you could alter the milk by using nonfat milk and you can also use light cream cheese instead of full fat cheddar cheese. Instead of margarine, use butter. Add vegetables such as carrots or broccoli to make it more nutritious.

Chapter 2: Understanding Meal Prep

There is a very well-known quote that has been hovering around the ears of men and weapon since the early days "Failing to prepare, it Preparing to Fail"

Even though this sentence seems like a very simple collection of words, it actually holds a very deep and elaborate meaning. To explain, the sentence explicitly focuses on the fact that without proper preparation, it is pretty much confirmed that you won't be able to win any battles of your life. And we are not talking about battles with guns and ammos! Rather, we are talking about the daily battles which we face.

Going into an exam, going to give the next presidential speech and even deciding to go on a diet! Without proper preparation or practice, you are bound to fail in all of those.

Please do pardon my slightly pessimistic intro! I am not talking about these just to discourage, rather, I want you to understand just how important preparation is to any victory.

Incidentally, the same concept is very much true when it comes to cooking!
Meal Prepping is one of the most important, yet highly ignored aspect of any diet. And this is even more true for an individual who leads a very busy life and finds it rather difficult to take off some time in order to create healthy and edible meals.
That being said, in this introductory chapter, I will be going through the basics of Meal Prep and teach you, how you can properly set up everything for your Meal Prep journey.

106. Exploring the Meal Prepping Concept

Perhaps in the simplest term, the main objective of Meal Prepping is to essentially create a blueprint of how you are going to conduct and incorporate the diet that you are following. Even if you are not following a diet! You can create a rough meal plan for the whole week.
Dissecting the concept even further, we are able to get the definition below:
"Meal Prepping is the process of planning what you are going to eat (and how you are going to make it) ahead of time."

107. Why should one Meal Prep?

And if you are wondering as to why should pursue Meal Prep, well...

- It helps you to save a lot of money by allowing you to set up a rough estimate of your food budget ahead of time
- If allows you to stick to a healthy plan and eat as much healthy food as possible
- It minimizes food wastage
- It clears off the burden of "What you should cook next" and eases your mind, clearing it up of any food related stress.

- Prevent the wasting of time by letting you know exactly "What" you are going to eat and "When".
- Help you avoid monotony in your daily meal by spicing up the routine from time to time.

108. Preparing your Kitchen for Meal Prepping

If you are jumping into the world of Meal Prep for the first time you might feel a bit confused as how you should prepare your kitchen.
These are some of the staple that you should keep around in your kitchen.

Cutting Boards: Try to get boards that are made from solid materials such as plastic, glass, rubber or marble! These are mostly corrosion resistant and the non-porous surface makes it easier to clean them than wood.
Tools and Equipment: the most basic ones include

Measuring cups: Required to measure out spices and condiments.
Various sized spoons: The multiple sized spoons will allow you to measure out small amounts of spices.

Glass bowls and non-metallic containers: They are required for storing the meat alongside marinade.
Packaging materials (mentioned above): The materials are mentioned above and they can be used to store the meat in the fridge.
Kitchen and paper towels: These are required draining the meat.
Cold Storage Space (fridge will suffice): Since the meats are required to be kept under 40-degree Fahrenheit, a fridge should be enough.

Knives: Sharp knives should be used to slice the meat accordingly. While using the knife, you should keep the following in mind.
- Always make sure to use a sharp knife

- Never hold a knife under your arm or leave it under a piece of meat
- Always keep your knives within visible distance
- Always keep your knife point down
- Always cut down towards the cutting surface and away from your body
- Never allow children to toy with knives unattended
- Wash the knives while cutting different types of food

Mesh glove for protection: Cutting the meat requires precision as you will be using a very sharp knife. The following types of glove should be kept in mind:
- **Rubber gloves**
- **Butchering Gloves**
- **Mesh Glove**

Kitchen Scale for measurement: A kitchen scale will allow you to get accurate measurements of slightly pieces of meat and condiments.

Internal Thermometer: A meat thermometer will help you to measure the internal temperature of the jerky to ensure that you are able to ensure that the jerky are ready.

Baking Sheet: These are flat, rectangular metal pan that are used in oven, mainly for flat products such as sheet cakes, cookies etc.

Colander: A colander is a bowl-shaped kitchen utensil with holes that allows you to drain food such as pasta or rice. These are also use to rinsed veggies.

Aluminum Foil: Also known as misnomer tin foil, these are used to wrap up and cover food.

109. The Different Time Saving Cooking Methods

If you don't buy expensive appliances such as the Instant Pot, Air Fryer or Crock Pot, the following cooking methods should help you to stay ahead of the pack and save a lot of time.

- **Grilling:** This method is best use when cooking tender cuts of fish or meat. The grill should be well heated before cooking. Some meats such as bacon, sausage already contain enough fat for grilling, for other cuts such as chicken breast, you will need to baste them with a bit of oil or cooking liquid.

- **Griddling:** This is also known as "Char-Grilling" and the method requires the user to cook in a ridged cast-iron pan on high heat that quickly sears the food on the outside. This method is not only fast, but healthy as well! Griddling is ideal for thin cuts such as chops, poultry breast fillets, steaks, seafood as well as thick slices of summer veggies such as zucchini or eggplant.
- **Stir Frying:** Lean cuts are perfect for stir frying as are other firm textured fish and shellfish noodle, rice and vegetables. Since this process allows for quick cooking, all the color, nutrients and flavor of the ingredients are preserved almost to perfection.
- **Steaming:** Food is steamed above simmering water. In this case, the natural flavor, shape, color and texture alongside all water-soluble vitamins and minerals are retained perfectly.
- **Microwaving:** While microwave may have an ill reputation amongst foodies, every kitchen needs one! If you are busy, foods can be prepared or re-heated in a fraction of the time it would take to cook following other conventional methods.
-

110. Amazing Meal Prep Ideas

Keep in mind that the following are just few of the hundreds of different Meal Prep ideas you can scrape up from the deepest corners of your brain! These are to merely give you an idea of what you can truly do and how you can start organizing your dietary regime.

Plan ahead of time: This is really important and the first step that you should do when practicing meal prep is to make a habit of planning your meals as early as possible. Early on, it is best recommended that you create meal plans of perhaps 2-3 days and increase the number as you become more experienced.

Keep a good supply of mason jars: When considering healthy salad, Mason jars are absolutely amazing! It is a good idea to prepare your salad and store them in mason jars ahead of time. While doing this though, make sure to keep the salad dressing at the bottom as they might make the greens soggy.

Three-way seasoning in one pan: If your diet requires you to stick with lean meats such as chicken, then seasoning them from time to time might become somewhat of a chore. A simple solution to that is to prepare a pan with aluminum foil dividers. Using these will allow you to season three or more (depending on how many dividers you are using) types of chicken seasoning to be done using the same pan!

Boil eggs in an oven instead of a pot: Boiling an egg following the traditional method is a lengthy and slow process, a good way to boil a bunch of eggs is to use your oven! Take a muffin tin and rimmed baking sheet and fill it up with water, add a dozen of eggs and boil them all in one go!

Keep your prepared smoothies frozen in muffin tins: Plopping out a number of different ingredients early in the morning might be a chore for some people. A simple solution to that is to go ahead and freeze up your blended smoothies in muffin tins. This will not only save up time, but will also give you a delicious dose of satisfaction as you wake up in the morning and toss a few "smoothie cups" into the blender for a simple yet healthy breakfast.

Roast vegetables that require the same time in one batch: If your meal plan requires a large number of veggies to be prepared, divide the veggies according to the time taken for them boil/roast and prepare the veggies in the same batch in one go! For example, you can create a batch of rapid cooking vegetables such as mushrooms, asparagus or cherry tomatoes and a batch of slow roasting vegies such as potatoes, cauliflowers and carrots in order to minimize time loss and maximize output. This will save a lot of time and make things more efficient.

Learn to effectively use a skewer: When you think of skewers, you automatically think of kabobs! But Skewers aren't necessarily designed to be used only with street meats. Wooden skewers can actually help you to measure how much meat you are going to consume in one go. So, you can punch in your meat in multiple skewers and divide them evenly and store them for the rest of the week. When the time comes, just take out one skewer and cook it up!

Keep a good supply of sectioned plastic containers: Containers are extremely important it comes to meal prepping! Keep as many as you can, and if possibly go for "Sectioned" ones as you will be able to keep the ingredients separated from each other in the same box. It will prevent making a mess and save space.

Keep a tab of your accomplishments: This is perhaps the most essential aspect of a Meal Prepping routine. Always make sure to somehow measure your progress and set small milestones for you to accomplish. Achieving these milestones will encourage you and inspire you further to keep pushing yourself until your reach your final goal. Alternatively, looking at your positive progress will greatly motivate you to push forward as well!

Chapter 3: Tips & Tricks for Meal Planning

111. Common Mistakes to Avoid

We all make mistakes; it is a part of human nature. But there are some common mistakes that are made by individuals during the early days of Meal Prepping.

To ensure that you do not make the same mistakes, let me outline a few!

- Don't keep your food for too long out as they might very easily get contaminated with germs of bacteria,
- Don't rush when washing and rinsing your vegetables. Putting a little time there won't destroy your daily routine! Take your time and thoroughly wash your vegies before processing them.
- You should always make sure that you are heating your foods properly. Overheating them will burn them up while not heating them enough will leave harmful bacteria on the surface of the

food. Use a meat thermometer if possible when dealing with meats.

112. Food Safety

Preventing contamination while handling the different ingredients is very important when it comes to prepping your ingredients for a meal plan!
Keeping that in mind, let me give you some times as to how you can keep your veggies and meat as safe and healthy as possible.

Vegetables: It is extremely important that you wash all of your vegetables and fruits before you eat them in order to ensure that the are safe to eat!
Washing will help you to remove bacteria that may have come with the vegetable as make it safe to eat.

Generally speaking, the bacteria are usually found in the soil where the veggie was grown, so you should wash in such a way so that no soil sticks to the body.
When washing the vegetables, wash them under a running tap and rub them well with the tap water.

A good way is to take a bowl of fresh water and rinse them thoroughly.
Make sure to start with the least soiled ones first and give them a final rinse before cooking.

Washing loose produces is particularly important as they tend to have more soil attached to them than pre-packed fruits and vegetables.
Another good way is to peel the skin off the fruits and veggies if possible to make them cleaner.

Asides from washing the veggies themselves, the following tips will help you to prevent cross contamination of vegetables
- Always make sure to wash your hands before handling raw food
- Store the raw food and the ones that are process separately

- Use different chopping foods for raw food and the ones that are processed for eating
- Make sure to always clean your knives

Meat: If you can make sure to follow the steps below, you will be able to ensure that your meat is safe from any kind of bacterial or airborne contamination.

This first step is very much essential as no market bought or freshly cut meat is completely sterile.

Following these, would greatly minimize the risk of getting affected by diseases.

- Make sure to properly wash your hand before beginning to process your meat. Use fresh tap water and soap/hand sanitizer.
- Make sure to remove any metal ornaments such as rings and watches from your wrist and hand before starting to handle the meat.
- Thoroughly clean the cutting surface using sanitizing liquid to remove any grease or unwanted contaminates. If you want to go for a homemade sanitizer, then you can simply make a solution of 1-part chlorine bleach and 10 parts water.
- The above-mentioned sanitizer should also be used to soak your tools such as knives and other equipment to ensure that they are safe to use as well.
- Alternatively, commercial acid based/ no rinsed sanitizer such as Star San will also work.
- After each and every use, all of the knives and other equipment such as meat grinders, slicers, extruders etc. should be cleaned thoroughly using soap water. The knives should be taken care in particular by cleaning the place just on top of the handle as it might contain blood and pieces of meat.
- When it comes to cleaning the surface, you should use cloths or sponges

Asides from the tips above, two other things that you should keep in mind are:

- You should always make sure that you keep store your meat in a place where the temperature is lower than 40-degree Fahrenheit as studies have shown that temperatures of 40-140-degree Fahrenheit provide optimal temperature for bacterial growth.

- If you are using pre-packed meat, then there remains a risk that the meat will eventually diminish after you open the package. However, this process can be significantly decelerated with the help of some excellent guidelines to cover your meat. (next section provides the rules)

113.   Simple guideline to cover and wrap your meat

- Using aluminum foil to cover up your meat will help to protect it from light and oxygen and keep the moisture intact. However, since Aluminum is reactive, it is advised that a layer of plastic wrap is used underneath the aluminum foil to provide double protective layer.
- If keeping the meat in a bowl with no lid, then a plastic wrap can be used to seal the bowl providing an air tight enclosure.
- Re-sealable bags provide protection by storing it in a bag and squeezing out any air.
- Airtight glass or plastic containers with lids are good option as well.
- A type of paper known as Freezer paper is specifically designed to wrap foods that are to be kept in the fridge. These wraps are amazing for meat as well.
- Vacuum sealers are often used for Sous Vide packaging. These machines are a bit expensive but are able to provide excellent packaging by completely sucking out any air from a re-sealable bag. This greatly increases the meats shelf life both outside and in the fridge.

114.   A Note on Sanitation

Keeping your cooking station clean should always be on the top of your priority list when cooking!
While cooking and experimenting with various ingredients, you will be dealing with different types of blemishes. Try to keep the following cleaners to help you deal with the different types of unnecessary materials:
- **Detergent/Dish Washing Liquid:** These are perfect for removing simple dust and surface oil.

- **Solvent Cleaners/Ammonia:** These contain grease-dissolving agents and help to clean similar materials.
- **Acid Cleaners as Hydrochloric Acid:** These contain grease-dissolving agents and help to clean similar materials.
- **Abrasive Cleaners:** These can clean materials such as fine steel, wool, nylon and copper
- **Solvent Cleaners/Ammonia:** These contain grease-dissolving agents and help to clean similar materials.
- **Sanitizers:** These are really good for cleaning the food preparation surface. These include:
  - ✓ Chlorine Bleach
  - ✓ Hydrogen Peroxide
  - ✓ White distilled vinegar

115. Tips to Prevent Cross-Contamination

Cross Contamination is one of the main reasons for food-borne diseases to spread! The following tips will help you to prevent such events from happening.

- Always wash your hand thoroughly with warm water. Also, the cutting boards, counters, knives and other utensils should also be cleaned as instructed at the first section of the chapter.
- Make sure to keep different types of meat in different bowls, dishes, and plates prior to using them.
- When storing the meat in fridge, make sure to keep the raw meat, seafood, poultry and eggs on the bottom shelf of your fridge and in individual sealed containers.
- Keep your refrigerator shelves cleaned and juices from meat/vegetables might drip on them.
- Always refrain yourself from keeping raw meat/vegetables in the same plate as cooked goods.
- Always make sure to clean your cutting boards and use different cutting boards for different types of foods. Raw meats, vegetables and other foods should not be cut using the same table.

116. FAQ

If this if your first time, then it's almost certain that you are going to have some questions regarding Meal Prep.

Let me clear some of the most common one's for you before letting you go into the recipes!

Q1. How long does stored food usually last?

As a rule of thumb, you should not store your food for more than 4 days in air tight containers.

Q2. How should you store meal prepped food?

A good way is to use plastic containers to store the cooked food. Make sure to allow your meals to cool for 30-40 minutes before sealing them though.

Q3. What does buffet meal prep mean?

A buffet meal prep is when you batch cook a number of different ingredients and then create meals during the week as you keep on going, instead of prepping all the meals at once.

Q4. What type of containers should you use?

Plastic containers are BPA free, microwave and dishwasher safe so these are really cool to use.

Q5. How should you motivate yourself to meal prep every week?

Good pointers to remember is that meal prep will help you to stay healthy, energy and maintain a very healthy physique! And most importantly, it will help you save up a lot of money.

Q6. Is Freezing good?

While freezing meals are not recommended (as re-heating them sometimes diminishes the flavor), you are more than welcome to chill sauces, soups, chilis etc. and thaw them when needed.

Q7. How are you to re-heat workweek lunches without ruining them?

When you are in the office, re-heat your meals using the office microwave, and while at home...try to re-heat your meal in oven or stove (it preserves the flavor almost perfectly)

And that pretty much covers the basics of Meal Prep! Now, let's dig deep into a step by step guide as to how you can actually prepare a healthy meal plan.

Chapter 4: Day 1 Meals

Thank you for allowing us to expose you to the large variety of Keto Meal Prep recipes that you can enjoy, please feel free to leave us a positive review if you like what you are about to read through.

BREAKFAST - AVOCADO WITH A HOLE

Yield: 6 Servings
Total Time: 20 Minutes
Prep Time: 5 Minutes
Cook Time: 15 Minutes

Ingredients:
- Avocados, cut in to half: 3
- Eggs:6
- Garlic powder: 1 teaspoon
- Salt: ½ teaspoon
- Black pepper: ¼ teaspoon
- Grated parmesan cheese: ¼ cup

Instructions:
Preheat your oven at 350 degrees Fahrenheit and cut your avocados in to half. Remove the pits from the avocados and remove about 1/3 of the meat from the avocados so that the egg can fit in. Put the avocados in to muffin tins with the sides facing up. Sprinkle over salt, black pepper and the garlic powder on the avocados. Break the egg over each avocado and sprinkle the grated parmesan cheese on top. Put the muffin tray to bake in the preheated oven for 10 to 15 minutes or until the egg is set properly. Enjoy!

Nutrition Information per Serving:
Calories: 261; Total Fat: 20 g; Carbs: 3 g; Dietary Fiber: 0 g;
Protein: 14 g; Cholesterol: 0 mg; Sodium: 0 mg

Lunch - Effective Low-Carb Sushi

Yield: 3
Total Time: 20 minutes
Prep Time: 10 minutes
Cooking Time: 10 minutes

Ingredients
- 16 ounces of cauliflower
- 6 ounce of softened cream cheese
- 1-2 tablespoon of Rice Vinegar
- 1 tablespoon of Soy Sauce
- 5 sheets of Nori
- 1 piece of 6-inch cucumber
- ½ a piece of medium Avocado
- 5 ounces of smoked salmon

Instructions
Open up the lid of your blender or food processor and add cauliflower. Pulse them until they turn into rice sized pieces. Slice up your cucumber on either side. Stand the cucumber and slice up the sides. Discard the middle part of the cucumber and keep the remaining 2 strips. Keep the cucumbers in your fridge. Take a skillet and heat up some oil over medium heat. Add your cauliflower and cook them well. Season with some soy sauce.

Transfer the cooked cauliflower to a bowl and add rice vinegar and cream cheese. Mix well. Let it chill in your fridge. Slice about ½ of your avocado and scoop out a bit of the flesh. Take your nori sheet down a bamboo roller and cover it up with saran wrap.
Spread out some cauliflower rice over your nori sheets and add in the fillings (cucumber, avocado, smoked salmon etc.) according to your desire. Roll up the sheets and serve!

Nutritional Information per Serving

Calories: 102; Total Fat: 3 g; Carbs: 10 g; Dietary Fiber: 2 g;
Protein: 9 g; Cholesterol: 7 mg; Sodium: 542 mg

DINNER - POPPY SEED CUPCAKE

Yield: 4
Total Time: 35 minutes
Prep Time: 10 minutes
Cooking Time: 25 minutes

Ingredients

- 3/4 cup of Blanched Almond flour
- ¼ cup of Golden Flaxseed Meal
- 1/3 cup of Erythritol
- 1 teaspoon of baking powder
- 2 tablespoons of Poppy Seeds
- ¼ cup of molten salted butter
- ¼ cup of heavy cream
- 3 large sized eggs
- Zest of 2 lemons
- 3 tablespoon of lemon juice
- 1 teaspoon of vanilla extract
- 25 drops of liquid stevia

Instructions

Pre-heat your oven to 350-degree Fahrenheit. Take a mixing bowl and add poppy seeds, almond flour and Erythritol. Add Flaxseed meal and stir. Add melted butter.
Pour heavy cream and egg, mix well to incorporate everything. Pour the batter into cupcake molds and bake for 20 minutes until you have a brown texture. Allow them to cool for 10 minutes. Enjoy!

Nutritional Information per Serving

Calories: 229; Total Fat: 15 g; Carbs: 18 g; Dietary Fiber: 1 g;
Protein: 6 g; Cholesterol: 77 mg; Sodium: 55 mg

Chapter 5: Day 2 Meals

Breakfast - Bacon, cheese and egg cups

Yield: 12 Servings
Total Time: 20 Minutes
Prep Time: 5 Minutes
Cook Time: 15 Minutes

Ingredients
- Eggs:12
- Frozen spinach: ½ cup
- Bacon strips: 12
- Cheddar cheese: 1/3 cup
- Salt: a pinch
- Pepper: a pinch

Instructions
Preheat your oven at 400 degrees Fahrenheit. Fry the bacon strips until they are crispy and set aside. Grease a muffin tray with oil and then place the fried bacon strips inside. In a bowl, mix together the eggs and beat well. Now add in the chopped spinach making sure it is dried properly. Pour the spinach and egg mixture in the muffin cases filling about ¾ of the muffin. Now sprinkle over the cheddar cheese and the salt and pepper. Bake in a preheated oven for 15 minutes or until the cheese has melted. Enjoy!

Nutritional Information per Serving
Calories: 101; Total Fat: 7 g; Carbs: 1 g; Dietary Fiber: 3 g; Protein: 8 g; Cholesterol: 30 mg; Sodium: 563 mg

LUNCH - CHEESY TUNA BITES

Yield: 4
Total Time: 20 minutes
Prep Time: 10 minutes
Cooking Time: 10 minutes

Ingredients

- 10 ounces of Drained up Canned Tuna
- ¼ cup of mayonnaise
- 1 cubed and medium sized Avocado
- ¼ cup of Parmesan Cheese
- 1/3 cup of Almond Flour
- ½ teaspoon of Garlic Powder
- ¼ teaspoon of Onion Powder
- Salt as needed
- Pepper as needed
- ½ a cup of Coconut Oil

Instructions

Take a small sized bowl and add the listed ingredients (except avocado and coconut oil). Fold the cubed avocado to the drained tuna and form a ball. Roll the balls in almond flour and cover. Place a skillet over medium-heat and add coconut oil, allow the oil to heat up. Add balls and fry the balls. Enjoy!

Nutritional Information per Serving

Calories: 273; Total Fat: 9 g; Carbs: 24 g; Dietary Fiber: 3 g;
Protein: 13 g; Cholesterol: 39 mg; Sodium: 436 mg

DINNER - MIGHTY CLOUD 9 CAKES

Yield: 8
Total Time: 45 minutes
Prep Time: 10 minutes
Cooking Time: 35 minutes

Ingredients
For the cake:
- 6 pieces of large separated large eggs
- 6 tablespoon of cream cheese at room temperature
- ½ a teaspoon of tartar cream
- 2 teaspoons of vanilla extract
- ¼ cup of granulated stevia

For the Frosting:
- 16 ounce of softened cream cheese
- 2 tablespoons of butter
- 1/3 cup of granulated stevia
- 1 tablespoon of vanilla extract

Instructions
Pre-heat your oven to a temperature of 300-degree Fahrenheit. Take a muffin tin and grease it up using cooking spray. Take another medium sized bowl and add cream cheese, egg yolks, sweetener, vanilla extract and mix everything until it has a nice and smooth consistency. Take another bowl and add egg whites and tartar cream. Mix them well until a foamy texture comes. Pour the whites into your egg mix.

Scoop 2 tablespoon of mix into your oven tins. Transfer the muffin tin to an oven and bake for 30 minutes. Take another bowl and add the frosting ingredients and beat using a mixer. Add the frosting to a pastry bag and add frosting on top of your muffin, add another muffin and top up with frosting followed by another muffin. Make three layers to prepare your cloud cake. Serve!

Nutritional Information per Serving *Calories: 275; Total Fat: 19 g; Carbs: 28 g; Dietary Fiber: 3 g; Protein: 10 g; Cholesterol: 150 mg; Sodium: 54 mg*

Chapter 6: Day 3 Meals

BREAKFAST - FAT BURNING VANILLA SMOOTHIE

Yield: 1 Servings
Total Time: 5 Minutes
Prep Time: 5 Minutes
Cook Time: 0 Minutes

Ingredients:
- Egg yolks: 2
- Mascarpone cheese: ½ cup
- Water: ¼ cup
- Ice cubes: 4
- Coconut oil: 1 tablespoon
- Vanilla extract: ½ teaspoon
- Liquid stevia: 3 drops
- Whipped cream: for topping

Instructions:
Take a blender, and add in the egg yolks, mascarpone cheese, water, ice cubes, coconut oil, vanilla extract and the liquid stevia and blend. Make sure that the ingredients are mixed well. Pour the mixture in to glasses. Top with whipped cream and enjoy!

Nutritional Information per Serving
Calories: 650; Total Fat: 64 g; Carbs: 4 g; Dietary Fiber: 3 g;
Protein: 12 g; Cholesterol: 9 mg; Sodium: 336 mg

LUNCH - PEANUT BUTTER CHOCOLATE BITES

Yield: 8
Total Time: 100 minutes
Prep Time: 90 minutes
Cooking Time: 10 minutes

Ingredients

- ½ a cup of cacao butter
- ½ a cup of salted peanut butter
- 3 tablespoons of stevia
- 4 tablespoon of powdered coconut milk
- 2 teaspoons of vanilla extract

Instructions

Set your double boiler on low-heat. Melt the cacao butter and peanut butter together and stir in vanilla extract. Take another bowl and add powdered coconut powder and stevia. Stir 1 tablespoon at a time of the mixture into the vanilla extract mixture. Portion the mixture into silicone molds or lined up muffin tins and chill them for 90 minutes. Remove and enjoy!

Nutritional Information per Serving

Calories: 135; Total Fat: 11 g; Carbs: 9 g; Dietary Fiber: 3 g; Protein: 3 g; Cholesterol: 0 mg; Sodium: 5 mg

DINNER - NO-BIG DEAL RASPBERRY POPSICLE

Yield: 6
Total Time: 120 minutes
Prep Time: 120 minutes
Cooking Time: 0 minutes

Ingredients
- 3 and a ½ ounce of Raspberries
- Juice of ½ a lemon
- ¼ cup of coconut oil
- 1 cup of coconut milk
- ¼ cup of sour cream
- ¼ cup of heavy cream
- ½ a teaspoon of Guar Gum
- 20 drops of Liquid Stevia

Instructions
Take an immersion blender and toss in all of the ingredients and blend them altogether nicely. Once done, take them mixture through a mesh and strain the mixture, discarding all of the raspberry seeds. Pour in the mixture into a mold and keep the mold inside the fridge for 2 hours. Once done, pass the mold through hot water to dislodge the popsicles.

Nutritional Information per Serving
Calories: 65; Total Fat: 1 g; Carbs: 11 g; Dietary Fiber: 1 g; Protein: 3 g; Cholesterol: 3 mg; Sodium: 41 mg

Chapter 7: Day 4 Meals

Thank you for allowing us to expose you to the large variety of Keto Meal Prep recipes that you can enjoy, please feel free to leave us a positive review if you like what you are about to read through.

BREAKFAST - BLACKBERRY KETO EGG BAKE

Yield: 4 Servings
Total Time: 25 Minutes
Prep Time: 10 Minutes
Cook Time: 15 Minutes

Ingredients:

- Egg: 5
- Butter: 1 tablespoon
- Coconut flour: 3 tablespoons
- Grated ginger: 1 teaspoon
- Vanilla: ¼ teaspoon
- Salt: 1/3 teaspoon
- Orange zest: ½
- Chopped rosemary: 1 teaspoon
- Fresh blackberries: ½ cup

Instructions:

Preheat your oven at 350 degrees Fahrenheit. Take a blender, and add in the eggs, butter, coconut flour, grated ginger, vanilla, salt and the orange zest and blend properly. Then add in the rosemary and blend. Pour the mixture in to muffin cups and then top each muffin with few blackberries. Put the muffin tray to bake in the preheated oven for 15 minutes or until the eggs are set. Enjoy!

Nutritional Information per Serving

Calories: 144; Total Fat: 10 g; Carbs: 2 g; Dietary Fiber: 5 g;
Protein: 8.5 g; Cholesterol: 58 mg; Sodium: 663 mg

LUNCH - SAUSAGE CASSEROLE

Yield: 6
Total Time: 40 minutes
Prep Time: 10 minutes
Cooking Time: 30 minutes

Ingredients
- 1 pound of pork sausage
- 2 cups of diced up zucchini
- 2 cups of shredded green cabbage
- ½ a cup of diced up onion
- 3 pieces of large eggs
- ½ a cup of mayonnaise
- 2 teaspoons of yellow mustard
- 1 teaspoon of dried ground sage
- 1 and a ½ cup of shredded and divided cheddar cheese
- Cayenne pepper as required

Instructions
Pre-heat your oven to 375-degree Fahrenheit. Take a casserole dish and grease it well.

Take a large sized skillet and place it over medium heat, add sausages and cook until you have a brown texture. Add zucchini, cabbages, onion and cook until tender. Remove the heat and spoon the mixture into casserole dish, keep it on the side.

Take a mixing bowl and add whisked eggs, mayonnaise, sage, pepper and mix. Add 1 cup of grated cheese into the egg mix and stir. Transfer the mix to the casserole and top with any remaining cheese. Place the casserole in the oven and bake for 30 minutes. Once the cheese has melted, remove and serve hot!

Nutritional Information per Serving
Calories: 300; Total Fat: 26 g; Carbs: 5 g; Dietary Fiber: 2 g;
Protein: 12 g; Cholesterol: 62 mg; Sodium: 576 mg

DINNER - JUICY PUMPKIN SPICE CAKES

Yield: 5
Total Time: 25 minutes
Prep Time: 10 minutes
Cooking Time: 15 minutes

Ingredients

- ¾ cup of canned of pumpkin
- ¼ of cup of organic seed butter
- 1 large of egg at room temperature
- 1/ cup of Erythritol
- ¼ cup of sifted organic coconut flour
- 2 tablespoon of organic flaxseed meal
- 1 teaspoon of ground cinnamon
- ½ a teaspoon of ground nutmeg
- ½ a teaspoon of baking soda
- ½ teaspoon of baking powder
- ¼ teaspoon of salt

Instructions

Pre-heat your oven to 350-degree Fahrenheit. Take a muffin tin and grease it up. Take a mixing bowl and add sunflower seed, butter, egg and pumpkin. Stir well until you have a nice and consistent mixture. Add the remaining ingredients and mix well.

Add 1 scoop of the mixture to your muffin tin, keep repeating until all of the mixture is used up. Bake the muffins for 15 minutes. Remove and top with cheese. Enjoy!

Nutritional Information per Serving

Calories: 337; Total Fat: 16 g; Carbs: 28 g; Dietary Fiber: 2 g;
Protein: 5 g; Cholesterol: 75 mg; Sodium: 137 mg

Chapter 8: Day 5 Meals

BREAKFAST - KETO COCONUT PANCAKES

Yield: 2 Servings
Total Time: 18 Minutes
Prep Time: 10 Minutes
Cook Time: 8 Minutes

Ingredients:
- Eggs: 2
- Cream cheese: 2 oz
- Almond flour: 1 tablespoon
- Cinnamon: 1 teaspoon
- Erythritol: ½ tablespoon
- Salt: a pinch
- Shredded coconut: ¼ cup
- Maple syrup: 4 tablespoons

Instructions:
Beat together the eggs in a bowl and then add in the cream cheese and the almond flour. Next add in the cinnamon, erythritol and the salt. Mix properly and then pour some of the batter in to a frying pan and fry the pancakes on both sides properly. Put in to a plate and sprinkle over the shredded coconut and then the maple syrup. Enjoy!

Nutritional Information per Serving
Calories: 575; Total Fat: 51 g; Carbs: 3.5 g; Dietary Fiber: 3 g;
Protein: 19 g; Cholesterol: 93 mg; Sodium: 346 mg

Lunch - Cinnamon and Almond Butter Smoothie

Yield: 1
Total Time: 2 minutes
Prep Time: 2 minutes
Cooking Time: 0 minutes

Ingredients
- 1 and a ½ cups of almond milk
- 1 scoop of collagen peptides
- 2 tablespoons of almond butter
- 2 tablespoons of golden flax meal
- ½ a teaspoon of cinnamon
- 15 drops of liquid stevia
- 1/8 teaspoon of almond extract
- 1/8 teaspoon of salt
- 6-8 ice cubes

Instructions
Add all of the ingredients to your blender and blend well until smooth. Allow them it to chill and enjoy!

Nutritional Information per Serving
Calories: 395; Total Fat: 24 g; Carbs: 17 g; Dietary Fiber: 2 g;
Protein: 13 g; Cholesterol: 0 mg; Sodium: 269 mg

DINNER - FEISTY CHOCOLATE AND PEANUT TARTS

Yield: 6
Total Time: 40 minutes
Prep Time: 10 minutes
Cooking Time: 30 minutes

Ingredients
For the Crust:
- ¼ cup of Flaxseed
- 2 tablespoons of Almond Flour
- 1 tablespoon of Erythritol
- 1 Large Egg White

For the Top Layer:
- 1 Medium sized Avocado
- 4 tablespoons of Cocoa Powder
- ¼ cup of Erythritol
- ½ teaspoon of vanilla extract
- ½ teaspoon of Cinnamon
- 2 tablespoons of Heavy Cream

Middle Layer:
- 4 tablespoons of Peanut Butter
- 2 tablespoons of butter

Instructions
Preheat our oven to a temperature of 350F. Take a separate bowl and toss in the flaxseed and grind them until they are firmly grounded. To the flaxseed mix, add up the rest of the ingredients listed under crust. Take a tart pan and pour down the crust mixture and put it inside the oven and bake it for 8 minutes. Take another bowl and prepare the top layer by combining all of the ingredients listed under crust and blend them to get a creamy and smooth mixture.

Once the curst inside the oven is complete, take it out and let it cool. For the peanut butter layer, you are going to need to take another bowl and melt the peanut butter and butter mixture in your microwave. Gently pour down the molten Peanut butter mixture on top of your crust letter and leave it for 30 minutes to settle down. Over the Peanut Butter layer, pour down the chocolate avocado layer and let the whole tart refrigerate for an hour. Take It out from the fridge and serve them well.

Nutritional Information per Serving
Calories: 264; Total Fat: 21 g; Carbs: 17 g; Dietary Fiber: 2 g;
Protein: 5 g; Cholesterol: 36 mg; Sodium: 53 mg

Chapter 9: Day 6 Meals

BREAKFAST - 5 INGREDIENT CHOCOLATE CHIP WAFFLES

Yield: 2 Servings
Total Time: 14 Minutes
Prep Time: 8 Minutes
Cook Time: 6 Minutes

Ingredients:
- Protein powder: 2 scoops
- Eggs, separated: 2
- Butter: 2 tablespoons
- Salt: a pinch
- Cacao nibs: 50 grams
- Maple syrup: ½ cup

Instructions
Beat the egg whites until stiff peaks form. In another bowl, mix the egg yolks, protein powder and the butter. Now fold in the egg whites in to this mixture. Now add in the salt and the cacao nibs. Mix well. Pour this mixture in to a waffle maker and cook until it turns golden brown on both sides. Serve warm and drizzle over maple syrup!

Nutritional Information per Serving
Calories: 400; Total Fat: 26 g; Carbs: 4.5 g; Dietary Fiber: 2 g;
Protein: 13 g; Cholesterol: 89 mg; Sodium: 358 mg

LUNCH - HEALTHY GREEN LOW- CARB SMOOTHIE

Yield: 1
Total Time: 5 minutes
Prep Time: 5 minutes
Cooking Time: 0 minutes

Ingredients
- 2 cups of spinach
- 1 and a ½ cups of ice
- 1 cup of almond milk
- ½ of avocado, chopped and pitted
- 1/4 cup of vanilla protein powder
- ¼ cup of stevia

Instructions
Add milk, spinach and the remaining ingredients to a blender. Blend until a nice texture form. Add some or ice or milk if needed. Pour into large glass and serve!

Nutritional Information per Serving
Calories: 225; Total Fat: 9 g; Carbs: 20 g; Dietary Fiber: 2 g;
Protein: 7 g; Cholesterol: 0 mg; Sodium: 155 mg

DINNER - SENSIBLE ORANGE AND COCONUT CREAMSICLE

Yield: 10
Total Time: 190 minutes
Prep Time: 10 minutes
Cooking Time: 180 minutes

Ingredients
- ½ a cup of coconut oil
- ½ a cup of heavy whipping cream
- 4 ounce of cream cheese
- 1 teaspoon of orange vanilla Mio
- 10 drops of liquid stevia

Instructions
Take an immersion blender and mix in all of the ingredients and blend them up. Take the mixture and pour it into the silicone tray and let it freeze for about 2-3 hours. Once it is hardened properly, finely remove the silicone tray and eat it up.

Nutritional Information per Serving
Calories: 245; Total Fat: 3 g; Carbs: 20 g; Dietary Fiber: 1 g;
Protein: 4 g; Cholesterol: 12 mg; Sodium: 529 mg

Chapter 10: Day 7 Meals

Thank you for allowing us to expose you to the large variety of Keto Meal Prep recipes that you can enjoy, please feel free to leave us a positive review if you like what you are about to read through.

BREAKFAST - PEANUT BUTTER AND CHOCOLATE MUFFINS

Yield: 6 Servings
Total Time: 45 Minutes
Prep Time: 20 Minutes
Cook Time: 25 Minutes

Ingredients:
- Almond flour: 1 cup
- Erythritol: ½ cup
- Baking powder: 1 teaspoon
- Salt: a pinch
- Peanut butter: 1/3 cup
- Almond milk: 1/3 cup
- Eggs: 2
- Cacao nibs: ½ cup

Instructions:
Mix together the almond flour, erythritol, baking powder and the salt. Now add in the peanut butter, almond milk and the eggs. Mix well. Lastly fold in the cacao nibs and put the mixture in to muffin cases. Preheat your oven at 350 degrees Fahrenheit and put the muffin tray to bake in the preheated oven for 25 minutes or until the muffins are cooked. Serve and enjoy!

Nutritional Information per Serving
Calories: 265; Total Fat: 20.5 g; Carbs: 2 g; Dietary Fiber: 7 g;
Protein: 7.5 g; Cholesterol: 65 mg; Sodium: 645 mg

Lunch - Parsley And Garlic Chicken Breast

Yield: 4
Total Time: 50 minutes
Prep Time: 10 minutes
Cooking Time: 40 minutes

Ingredients
- 1 tablespoon of divided dry parsley
- 1 tablespoon of divided dry basil
- 4 skinless and boneless chicken breast halves
- 4 thinly sliced garlic cloves
- ½ a teaspoon of salt
- ½ a teaspoon of crushed red pepper flakes
- 2 sliced tomatoes

Instructions
Preheat your oven to 350-degree Fahrenheit. Take a 9x13 inch baking dish and grease with cooking spray. Sprinkle 1 tablespoon of parsley, 1 teaspoon of basil and spread over the baking dish. Arrange your chicken breast halves carefully in the dish. Sprinkle garlic slices on top. Take a small bowl and add 2 teaspoon of parsley, 2 teaspoons of basil, salt, red pepper and basil. Mix well and spread the mixture over the chicken
Top with tomato slices. Cover and bake for 25 minutes. Remove the cover and bake for 15 minutes more. Serve and enjoy!

Nutritional Information per Serving
Calories: 257; Total Fat: 17 g; Carbs: 2 g; Dietary Fiber: 1 g; Protein: 25 g; Cholesterol: 74 mg; Sodium: 144 mg

DINNER - PERSONAL PAN PIZZA

Yield: 4
Total Time: 20 minutes
Prep Time: 5 minutes
Cooking Time: 15 minutes

Ingredients

- 4 pieces of large sized Portobello Mushroom Caps
- 1 medium sized Vine Tomato
- 4 ounces of Fresh Mozzarella Cheese
- ¼ cup of Freshly Chopped up Basil
- 6 tablespoons of Olive Oil
- 20 slices of Pepperoni
- Salt as needed
- Pepper as needed

Instructions

Prepare the mushroom and scrap out the internals, making sure to keep only the shell. Turn the shells over and broil them. Coat the shell with 3 tablespoon of olive oil and season with salt and pepper. Broil for 5 minutes more. Slice the tomato to thin slices and place them on top of the mushroom. Garnish with fresh basil and add pepperoni, cubed cheese on top. Broil for 4 minutes more to melt the cheese. Serve and enjoy!

Nutritional Information per Serving

Calories: 227; Total Fat: 15 g; Carbs: 2 g; Dietary Fiber: 2 g;
Protein: 21 g; Cholesterol: 69 mg; Sodium: 301 mg

Chapter 11: Day 8 Meals

BREAKFAST - EASY BLENDER PANCAKES

Yield: 1 Servings
Total Time: 20 Minutes
Prep Time: 5 Minutes
Cook Time: 15 Minutes

Ingredients:
- Cream cheese: 2 oz
- Eggs: 2
- Protein powder: 1 scoop
- Cinnamon: a pinch
- Salt: a pinch

Instructions:
Take a blender and blend in the cream cheese, eggs, protein powder, cinnamon and the salt. Heat up a frying pan and put in the batter to fry the pancake. Cook the pancake on both sides. Serve when done!

Nutrition Information per Serving:
Calories 450 grams
Fat 29 grams
Protein 41 grams
Carbs 4 grams

Nutritional Information per Serving
Calories: 450; Total Fat: 29 g; Carbs: 4 g; Dietary Fiber: 3 g;
Protein: 41 g; Cholesterol: 0 mg; Sodium: 436 mg

LUNCH - SPICY HOT CHICKEN PEPPER SOUP

Yield: 4
Total Time: 15 minutes
Prep Time: 5 minutes
Cooking Time: 10 minutes

Ingredients

- 1 teaspoon of Coriander Seeds
- 2 tablespoons of Olive Oil
- 2 sliced chili pepper
- 2 cups of chicken broth
- 2 cups of water
- 1 teaspoon of Turmeric
- ½ a teaspoon of Ground Cumin
- 4 tablespoons of Tomato Paste
- 16 ounce of chicken thigh
- 2 tablespoons of butter
- 1 medium sized avocado
- 2 ounces of Queso Fresco
- 4 tablespoons of chopped up Cilantro
- Juice of a half lime
- Salt as required
- Pepper as required

Instructions

Cut the chicken thigh evenly into small portions. Take pan and place it over medium heat, add oil and allow the oil to heat up. Add chicken and brown them on both sides, transfer them to plate and keep them on the side. Add 2 tablespoon of olive oil to the pan and add coriander seeds, toast them until a nice fragrance comes. Add chili.

Pour water and broth and simmer over low heat. Season with turmeric, salt, pepper, ground cumin. Bring to simmer once again and add tomato paste and butter, stir well to combine. Simmer for 10 minutes and add juice. Add 4 ounce of chicken thigh pieces and mix well. Garnish with ¼ of avocado and serve with an ounce of cilantro and queso fresco. Enjoy!

Nutritional Information per Serving

Calories: 140; Total Fat: 4 g; Carbs: 17 g; Dietary Fiber: 1 g; Protein: 6 g; Cholesterol: 6 mg; Sodium: 185 mg

DINNER - SPECIALLY MADE STRAWBERRY MILKSHAKE

Yield: 2
Total Time: 5 minutes
Prep Time: 5 minutes
Cooking Time: 0 minutes

Ingredients
- ¾ cup of coconut milk
- ¼ cup of heavy cream
- 7 cubes of ice
- 2 tablespoons of sugar free Strawberry Torani
- 1-2 tablespoon of MCT Oil
- ¼ teaspoon of Xanthan Gum

Instructions
Take a blender and toss in all of the ingredients into the blender. Blend it for about 1-2 minutes until everything is finely mixed. Serve.

Nutritional Information per Serving
Calories: 192; Total Fat: 9 g; Carbs: 20 g; Dietary Fiber: 2 g;
Protein: 4 g; Cholesterol: 0 mg; Sodium: 8 mg

Chapter 12: Day 9 Meals

BREAKFAST - BUTTER COFFEE

Yield: 1 Servings
Total Time: 17 Minutes
Prep Time: 5 Minutes
Cook Time: 12 Minutes

Ingredients:
- Water: 1 cup
- Coffee: 2 tablespoons
- Grass fed butter: 1 tablespoon
- Coconut oil: 1 tablespoon

Instructions:
Take a sauce pan and boil in the water. Now add in the ground coffee, coconut oil and the grass-fed butter. Once boiled, pour in to a cup through a strainer to strain the bits and pieces. Enjoy while it is hot!

Nutritional Information per Serving
Calories: 230; Total Fat: 25 g; Carbs: 0 g; Dietary Fiber: 0 g;
Protein: 0 g; Cholesterol: 0 mg; Sodium: 0 mg

LUNCH - VERY LOW CARB CHICKEN SATAY

Yield: 2
Total Time: 10 minutes
Prep Time: 5 minutes
Cooking Time: 5 minutes

Ingredients
- 1 pound of Ground Chicken
- 4 tablespoons of Soy Sauce
- 2 springs of Onion
- 1/3 pieces of Yellow Pepper
- 1 tablespoon of Erythritol
- 1 tablespoon of Rice Vinegar
- 2 teaspoons of Sesame Oil
- 2 teaspoons of Chili Paste
- 1 teaspoon of Minced Garlic
- 1/3 teaspoon of Cayenne Pepper
- ¼ teaspoon of Paprika
- Juice of ½ a lime

Instructions
Add 2 teaspoon of sesame oil to a pan and heat it up over medium-high heat. Add the ground chicken to the pan and brown it for a while. Add the remaining ingredients and mix well, keep cooking. Once the mixture has reached your desired texture, add 2 chopped up spring and 1/3 of sliced yellow pepper. Mix well and serve hot!

Nutritional Information per Serving
Calories: 436; Total Fat: 15 g; Carbs: 5 g; Dietary Fiber: 3 g;
Protein: 67 g; Cholesterol: 199 mg; Sodium: 1605 mg

DINNER - SAUSAGE AND CHEESE BOWL

Yield: 1
Total Time: 40 minutes
Prep Time: 10 minutes
Cooking Time: 30 minutes

Ingredients

- 1 and a ½ of cheddar and bacon chicken sausage
- ¾ of cup grated cheddar cheese
- ¼ cup of coconut flour
- ¼ cup of coconut oil
- 2 tablespoon of coconut milk
- 5 pieces of egg yolks
- 2 teaspoons of Lemon Juice
- ½ a teaspoon of Rosemary
- ¼ teaspoon of Cayenne Pepper
- ¼ teaspoon of Baking Soda
- 1/8 teaspoon of Salt

Instructions

Cut the chicken sausage into bite sized portions. Take a skillet and place it over medium-high heat. Pre-heat your oven to 350-degree Fahrenheit. Separate the egg yolks and eggs, discard the whites. Take a bowl and measure out dry flour and spices and add them to the bowl. Take another bowl and add any dry ingredient and mix
Beat the eggs until frothy.

Pour the lemon juice, coconut oil, coconut milk to the egg and keep beating it. Pour the wet ingredients into the bowl with dry ingredients. Fold ½ a cup of your cheddar cheese into your batter. Prepare 2 ramekins and fill them up with ¾ of your batter. Give them a poke and bake the mix in your pre-heated oven for about 25 minutes. Serve!

Nutritional Information per Serving

Calories: 595; Total Fat: 39 g; Carbs: 18 g; Dietary Fiber: 2 g;
Protein: 43 g; Cholesterol: 477 mg; Sodium: 1132 mg

Chapter 13: Day 10 Meals

Thank you for allowing us to expose you to the large variety of Keto Meal Prep recipes that you can enjoy, please feel free to leave us a positive review if you like what you are about to read through.

BREAKFAST - DETOX TEA

Yield: 1 Servings
Total Time: 20 Minutes
Prep Time: 5 Minutes
Cook Time: 15 Minutes

Ingredients:
- Warm water: 1 cup
- Apple cider vinegar: 2 tablespoons
- Lemon juice: 2 tablespoons
- Honey: 1 tablespoon
- Cinnamon: 1 teaspoon
- Cayenne: a pinch

Instructions:
Take a cup, and add in the warm water, apple cider vinegar, lemon juice, honey, cinnamon and the cayenne and mix properly so that all the ingredients are mixed in properly. Enjoy while your tea is warm!

Nutritional Information per Serving
Calories: 84; Total Fat: 0 g; Carbs: 20 g; Dietary Fiber: 0 g; Protein: 0 g; Cholesterol: 3 mg; Sodium: 436 mg

LUNCH - FANCY BROWNIE

Yield: 5
Total Time: 45 minutes
Prep Time: 10 minutes
Cooking Time: 35 minutes

Ingredients
- 1 cup of Golden Flaxseed Meal
- ¼ cup of cocoa powder
- 1 tablespoon of Cinnamon
- ½ tablespoon of Baking Powder
- ½ a teaspoon of Salt
- 1 piece of large egg
- 2 tablespoons of Coconut Oil
- ¼ cup of Sugar free Caramel Syrup
- ½ a cup of Pumpkin Puree
- 1 teaspoon of Vanilla Extract
- 1 teaspoon of Apple Cider Vinegar
- ¼ cup of Silvered Almond

Instructions
Pre-heat your oven to 350-degree Fahrenheit. Take a mixing bowl and add the listed ingredients and mix well. Take desired number of muffin tins and line them up with paper liners. Scoop the batter into the muffin tins and fill them up into 1/4rth of liner
Sprinkle almond on top. Transfer to your oven and bake for 15 minutes. Serve and enjoy!

Nutritional Information per Serving
Calories: 241; Total Fat: 9 g; Carbs: 20 g; Dietary Fiber: 3 g;
Protein: 2 g; Cholesterol: 3 mg; Sodium: 126 mg

DINNER - SIMPLE SMALL TIME KIMCHI

Yield: 4
Total Time: 15 minutes
Prep Time: 5 minutes
Cooking Time: 10 minutes

Ingredients
For the Quick Kimchi:
- 3 cups of Purple Cabbage
- 3 tablespoons of Rice Vinegar
- 1 tablespoon of Minced up Garlic
- 2 teaspoons of minced Ginger
- 1 and a ½ tablespoon of Red Pepper Flakes
- 1/3 of a medium Daikon Radish
- 1 large sized Scallion
- 1 medium sized red Chili
- 1 tablespoon of Red Curry Paste
- 1 and a ½ tablespoon of Soy Sauce

For the Stir Fry:
- 1 pound of Pork Tenderloin
- 3 tablespoons of Coconut Oil
- 3 and a ½ ounce of Shitake Mushroom
- 1 large sized Scallion
- 2 tablespoons of White Wine
- 1 tablespoon of NOW Erythritol
- 2 tablespoons of Sesame Oil
- Salt as needed
- Pepper as needed

Instructions

Slice up the cabbage into fine strips. Slice up the radish into matchstick portions. Take a bowl and add the quick Kimchi ingredients to the bowl and mix them well. Take a pork loin and slice it up into ¼ inch thick medallions. Pour about 1 tablespoon of coconut oil to a pan and toss in half of the pork and cook it until brown spots appear on either side. Repeat for the other half. Pour in the wine, 1 tablespoon of coconut oil alongside the sesame oil. Toss in the chopped-up scallion and shiitake mushrooms and sauté them for about 5 minutes. Toss in the Kimchi to the same pan and let the juices boil up for about 4-5 minutes. Toss in the pork and cook for a few minutes extra to make sure everything is finely done.

Nutritional Information per Serving
Calories: 433; Total Fat: 24 g; Carbs: 30 g; Dietary Fiber: 2 g;
Protein: 11 g; Cholesterol: 60 mg; Sodium: 428 mg

Chapter 14: Day 11 Meals

BREAKFAST - SKILLET BAKED EGGS WITH YOGURT, CHILI OIL AND SPINACH

Yield: 4-6 Servings
Total Time: 30 Minutes
Prep Time: 15 Minutes
Cook Time: 15 Minutes

Ingredients:
- Greek yogurt: 2/3 cup
- Garlic clove: 1
- Butter: 2 tablespoons
- Olive oil: 2 tablespoons
- Chopped leak: 3 tablespoons
- Chopped scallions: 2 tablespoons
- Lemon juice: 1 teaspoon
- Fresh spinach: 10 cups
- Eggs: 4
- Turkish chili powder: ¼ teaspoon
- Chopped oregano: 1 teaspoon

Instructions:
In a bowl, mix the Greek yogurt, garlic and the salt and set it aside. Preheat your oven at 300 degrees Fahrenheit. On medium heat, add the olive oil in a skillet and fry in the chopped scallions and the chopped leak. Cook until they are soft. Now add in the spinach and the lemon juice. Cook for a few minutes and then create a hole between the skillet and very carefully break the eggs one by one in the center so as to not break the eggs.

Put the skillet in to the preheated oven to bake for 10 to 15 minutes or until the egg is set. In a frying pan, melt the butter and add in the Turkish chili powder and the oregano and cook. Drizzle over this spiced butter on the cooked eggs. Discard the garlic cloves from the yogurt and serve your baked eggs with yogurt.

Nutritional Information per Serving

Calories: 223; Total Fat: 14.1; Carbs: 12 g; Dietary Fiber: 9 g;
Protein: 11.1 g; Cholesterol: 78 mg; Sodium: 546 mg

LUNCH - CINNAMON CHOCOLATE SMOOTHIE

Yield: 2
Total Time: 5 minutes
Prep Time: 5 minutes
Cooking Time: 0 minutes

Ingredients

- ¾ cup of coconut milk
- ½ of a ripe avocado
- 2 teaspoon of unsweetened cacao powder
- 1 teaspoon of cinnamon powder
- ¼ teaspoon of vanilla extract
- Stevia as needed
- ½ a teaspoon of coconut oil

Instructions

Add all of the ingredients to your blender and blend well until smooth. Allow them it to chill and enjoy!

Nutritional Information per Serving

Calories: 98; Total Fat: 2 g; Carbs: 17 g; Dietary Fiber: 2 g; Protein: 2 g; Cholesterol: 6 mg; Sodium: 110 mg

DINNER - EASY MCGRIDDLE CASSEROLE

Yield: 8
Total Time: 55 minutes
Prep Time: 10 minutes
Cooking Time: 40 minutes

Ingredients

- 1 cup of almond flour
- ¼ cup of Flaxseed Meal
- 1 pound of breakfast sausage
- 10 large pieces of eggs
- 4 ounce of cheddar cheese
- 6 tablespoons of Walden Farms Maple Syrup
- 4 tablespoons of Butter
- ½ a teaspoon of Onion Powder
- ½ a teaspoon of Garlic Powder
- ¼ teaspoon of Sage
- Salt as required
- Pepper as required

Instructions

Pre-heat your oven to 350-degree Fahrenheit. Take a pan and place it over medium heat. Add sausage and cook them and break them apart. Take another bowl and add the dry ingredients. Add wet ingredients to the bowl and mix (except syrup). Add 4 tablespoon of syrup and mix again.

Pour the whole mixture over the cooked sausages and stir. Take a 9x9 inch casserole dish and prepare it using a parchment paper. Add the sausage mixture to the casserole and drizzle 2 tablespoon of syrup over. Bake for 45-50 minutes. Remove and enjoy!

Nutritional Information per Serving

Calories: 499; Total Fat: 39 g; Carbs: 16 g; Dietary Fiber: 2 g;
Protein: 24 g; Cholesterol: 302 mg; Sodium: 603 mg

Chapter 15: Day 12 Meals

BREAKFAST - BACON AND EGGS IN A DIFFERENT WAY

Yield: 3 Servings
Total Time: 40 Minutes
Prep Time: 10 Minutes
Cook Time: 30 Minutes

Ingredients:
- Full fat cream cheese: 100 grams
- Dried oregano thyme: ¼ teaspoon
- Large eggs: 6
- Bacon slices: 12

Instructions:
Preheat your oven at 400 degrees Fahrenheit. Take a bowl and mix together the full fat cream cheese with the dried oregano thyme and then set the bowl aside. Boil the eggs in a hot water sauce pan for 10 minutes. After that, peel the eggs and remove the egg yolks and set the egg yolks aside.

Fill the egg whites with the cream cheese filling in the egg yolk hole. Cover the egg with the rest of the egg white. Wrap the bacon slices tightly around the egg so that it in intact. Place the wrapped eggs in a baking dish and put to bake in preheated oven for 30 minutes. Remove from the oven and serve.

Nutritional Information per Serving
Calories: 205; Total Fat:17.2 g; Carbs: 0.7 g; Dietary Fiber: 3 g;
Protein: 11.9 g; Cholesterol: 24 mg; Sodium: 985 mg

LUNCH - SALMON AND SESAME GLAZED GINGER

Yield: 2
Total Time: 20 minutes
Prep Time: 10 minutes
Cooking Time: 10 minutes

Ingredients

- 10 ounces of Salmon Fillet
- 2 tablespoons of Soy Sauce
- 2 teaspoons of Sesame Oil
- 1 tablespoon of Rice Vinegar
- 1 teaspoon of Minced Ginger
- 2 teaspoons of Minced Garlic
- 1 tablespoon of Red boat Fish Sauce
- 1 tablespoon of Sugar Free Ketchup
- 2 tablespoons of Dry White Wine

Instructions

Add in all of the ingredients to a small sized Tupperware. Just make sure not to toss the sesame oil, white wine and ketchup. Marinade everything for about 10-15 minutes
Bring down the pan to a nice heat and toss in the sesame oil. One the smoke is seen, add the fish with the skin side down. Let it cook until crispy. Flip it and cook the other side. Each side should take about 3-4 minutes. Pour in the marinade liquid to the fish and let it boil. Slowly remove the fish from the pan and pour in the ketchup alongside the white wine to the liquid in the pan. Simmer for 5 minutes and serve as a side

Nutritional Information per Serving

Calories: 309; Total Fat: 22 g; Carbs: 2 g; Dietary Fiber: 1 g;
Protein: 25 g; Cholesterol: 102 mg; Sodium: 338 mg

DINNER - AMARETTO COOKIES

Yield: 4
Total Time: 45 minutes
Prep Time: 10 minutes
Cooking Time: 35 minutes

Ingredients

- 1 cup of Almond Flour
- 2 tablespoons of Coconut Flour
- ½ a teaspoon of Baking Powder
- ¼ a teaspoon of Cinnamon
- ½ a teaspoon of Salt
- ½ a cup of Erythritol
- 2 large sized eggs
- 4 tablespoons of Coconut Oil
- ½ a teaspoon of Vanilla Extract
- ½ a teaspoon of Almond Extract
- 2 tablespoons of Sugar-Free Jam
- 1 tablespoon of Organic Shredded Coconut

Instructions

Pre-heat your oven to 300-degree Fahrenheit. Take 2 muffin tins and grease them with non-stick spray. Take a bowl and add cream cheese, egg yolks, sweetener, and vanilla extract. Beat the mixture well until everything is incorporated well and you have a nice consistency. Take a separate bowl and add cream of tartar and egg whites. Mix it well using an electric mixer.

Carefully add the whipped mixture to the yolk mix. Scoop the mix into your prepared muffin tins. Place the muffin tins in your oven and bake for about 30-35 minutes. Once done, let the muffins cool in a cooling rack. Take a medium sized pan and add all of the ingredients listed under frosting. Beat the mixture well using a mixer. Fill up the frosting in a bag and carefully whip the muffin and decorate them with three layers. Serve and enjoy!

Nutritional Information per Serving

Calories: 456; Total Fat: 32 g; Carbs: 39 g; Dietary Fiber: 2 g;
Protein: 4 g; Cholesterol: 61 mg; Sodium: 58 mg

Chapter 16: Day 13 Meals

Thank you for allowing us to expose you to the large variety of Keto Meal Prep recipes that you can enjoy, please feel free to leave us a positive review if you like what you are about to read through.

BREAKFAST - LOW CARB CREAM CHEESE PANCAKES

Yield: 4 Servings
Total Time: 20 Minutes
Prep Time: 10 Minutes
Cook Time: 15 Minutes

Ingredients
- Cream cheese: 2 oz
- Eggs: 2
- Granulated sugar: 1 teaspoon
- Ground cinnamon: ½ teaspoon
- Butter: 2 tablespoons

Instructions
Take a blender and add in the cream cheese, eggs, granulated sugar and the ground cinnamon. Melt the butter in to a frying pan and pour spoonful's from the batter on to the frying pan. Flip the pancake to the other side to make sure that the pancake is cooked from both sides. Repeat the process with the remaining batter. Serve your pancakes with fresh fruit, berries or sugar free syrup.

Nutritional Information per Serving
Calories: 344; Total Fat: 29 g; Carbs:3 g; Dietary Fiber: 5 g; Protein: 17 g; Cholesterol: 56 mg; Sodium: 616 mg

LUNCH - GENEROUS POPPER MUG CAKE

Yield: 2
Total Time: 10 minutes
Prep Time: 5 minutes
Cooking Time: 5 minutes

Ingredients
- 2 tablespoons of Almont Flour
- 1 tablespoon of Golden Flaxseed Meal
- 1 tablespoon of Butter
- 1 tablespoon of Cream Cheese
- 1 large side Egg
- 1 sliced and cooked bacon
- ½ of a Jalapeno Pepper
- ½ teaspoon of Baking Powder
- ¼ teaspoon of Salt

Instructions
Take a frying pan and place it over medium heat. Add slice bacon and cook until they have a nice texture. Take a microwave proof container and mix all of the listed ingredients, including the bacon and Microwave for 75 seconds. Take the cup out and slam it against a surface to take the cake out. Garnish with jalapeno and serve!

Nutritional Information per Serving
Calories: 423; Total Fat: 20 g; Carbs: 6.5 g; Dietary Fiber: 4 g;
Protein: 6 g; Cholesterol: 31 mg; Sodium: 387 mg

DINNER - CRAZY BACON BURGER BOMBS

Yield: 12
Total Time: 70 minutes
Prep Time: 10 minutes
Cooking Time: 60 minutes

Ingredients

- 12 slices of bacon
- 12 cubes of 1-inch sized smoked cheddar cheese
- 12 rounds of 1-ounce raw sausage patties
- Salt as needed
- Cumin as needed
- Onion powder as needed
- Pepper as needed

Instructions

Pre-heat your oven to a temperature 350-degree Fahrenheit. Lay your sausage rounds on a cookie sheet lined up with parchment paper. Dust the sausages with onion powder, cumin, pepper and salt. Add pieces of cheese in the middle part of your rounds

Form a ball all around the cheese with sausage and roll them up using in hand, giving them a firm shape. Wrap the bacon around your sausage balls. Bake for about 60 minutes at 350-degree Fahrenheit. Have fun eating!

Nutritional Information per Serving

Calories: 312; Total Fat: 16 g; Carbs: 25 g; Dietary Fiber: 3 g;
Protein: 11 g; Cholesterol: 21 mg; Sodium: 538 mg

Chapter 17: Day 14 Meals

BREAKFAST - SMOKED SALMON AND EGG STUFFED AVOCADOS

Yield: 4 Servings
Total Time: 20 Minutes
Prep Time: 5 Minutes
Cook Time: 15 Minutes

Ingredients:

- Avocados: 4
- Smoked salmon: 4 oz
- Eggs: 8
- Salt- ½ teaspoon
- Black pepper: ¼ teaspoon
- Chili flakes: ¼ teaspoon
- Fresh dill: 2 tablespoons

Instructions:

Preheat your oven to 425 degrees Fahrenheit. Slice your avocados in to half and then scoop out its seed large enough for the egg to fit in. Take a baking sheet and place the smoked salmon slices on the sheet. Place the halved avocados on the sheet. In a bowl, beat the eggs and then put in the beaten egg in the avocado hole. Sprinkle salt and pepper on to the avocado. Put the tray to bake in the preheated oven for about 15 to 20 minutes. Sprinkle over some chili flakes and fresh dill on to the avocados and then serve warm!

Nutritional Information per Serving

Calories: 480; Total Fat: 10 g; Carbs: 18 g; Dietary Fiber: 14 g;
Protein: 20 g; Cholesterol: 93 mg; Sodium: 346 mg

LUNCH - EASY TO MAKE SHRIMP CURRY

Yield: 2
Total Time: 15 minutes
Prep Time: 5 minutes
Cooking Time: 10 minutes

Ingredients

- 2 tablespoon of Green Curry paste
- 1 cup of vegetable stock
- 1 cup of coconut milk
- 6 ounces of Pre-Cooked shrimp
- 5 ounce of Broccoli florets
- 3 tablespoons of chopped Cilantro
- 2 tablespoons of Coconut Oil
- 1 tablespoon of Soy Sauce
- ½ of a lime juice
- 1 medium sized spring onion chopped up
- 1 teaspoon of crushed roasted garlic
- 1 teaspoon of minced garlic
- 1 teaspoon of fish sauce
- ½ teaspoon of Turmeric
- ¼ teaspoon of Xanthan Gum
- ½ of a cup of source cream

Instructions

Place a pan over medium heat and add 2 tablespoon of coconut oil. Add minced ginger, chopped onion and cook for a minute. Add turmeric and curry paste. Add a tablespoon of soy sauce and fish sauce and give it a nice mix. Add a cup of vegetable stock alongside a cup of coconut milk. Stir well and add the green curry paste, simmer well.

Add ¼ teaspoon of Xanthan Gum and give it a nice stir. Once the curry begins to thicken, add florets and stir well. Add fresh chopped cilantro and stir until you have a good consistency, add the pre-cooked shrimp and lime juice. Mix and simmer for a few minutes. Season with pepper and salt and serve with sour cream. Enjoy!

Nutritional Information per Serving
Calories: 239; Total Fat: 17 g; Carbs: 7 g; Dietary Fiber: 1 g; Protein: 17 g; Cholesterol: 143 mg; Sodium: 652 mg

DINNER - EVERYBODY LOVES A PORK BITE

Yield: 3
Total Time: 55 minutes
Prep Time: 15 minutes
Cooking Time: 40 minutes

Ingredients
- 10 ounce of thin pork belly strips
- 1 tablespoon of butter
- ¼ of a large diced onion
- 2 ounces of blue cheese
- 4 tablespoon of heavy whipping cream
- 1 teaspoon of salt
- Pepper as needed

Instructions
Pre-heat your oven to 250-degree Fahrenheit. Transfer the pork belly strips to a baking dish. Season with salt and cover the belly strips in a thin layer of salt. Transfer them to your oven and cook for 30-45 minutes. Take a pan and place it over medium heat

Add butter and allow the butter to melt. Add onion and Saute for a few minutes, add blue cheese and allow it to melt. Pour the melted dish over the baked pork strips.

Cut into bite sized portion and serve!

Nutritional Information per Serving
Calories: 602; Total Fat: 38 g; Carbs: 19 g; Dietary Fiber: 1 g;
Protein: 50 g; Cholesterol: 137 mg; Sodium: 975 mg

Chapter 18: Day 15 Meals

Breakfast - Mocha chia pudding

Yield: 2 Servings
Total Time: 35 Minutes
Prep Time: 5 Minutes
Cook Time: 30 Minutes

Ingredients:
- Herbal coffee: 2 tbsp.
- Water: 2 cups
- Dry chia seeds: 55 grams
- Coconut cream: 1/3 grams
- Vanilla extract: 1 tablespoon
- Swerve: 1 tbsp.
- Cacao nibs: 2 tbsp.

Instructions:
Brew the herbal coffee by cooking the herbal coffee powder and the water and cook until the liquid is reduced to half. Strain the coffee and then mix in the coconut cream, vanilla extract and the swerve. Now add in the cacao nibs and the dry chia seeds. Pour the coffee in to cups and then refrigerate them for 30 minutes. When serving, sprinkle cacao nibs over the pudding before serving.

Nutritional Information per Serving
Calories: 257; Total Fat: 20.3g; Carbs: 2.4 g; Dietary Fiber: 3 g;
Protein: 13 g; Cholesterol: 39 mg; Sodium: 436 mg

LUNCH - DELIGHTFULLY CRUSTED SALMON DISH

Yield: 2
Total Time: 13 minutes
Prep Time: 5 minutes
Cooking Time: 8 minutes

Ingredients

- ½ a cup of walnuts
- 2 tablespoon of sugar free maple syrup
- ½ a tablespoon of Dijon Mustard
- ¼ teaspoon of Dill
- 2 pieces of 3-ounce Salmon Fillets
- 1 tablespoon of Olive Oil
- Salt as needed
- Pepper as needed

Instructions

Pre-heat your oven to 350-degree Fahrenheit. Add walnuts, mustard and maple syrup to the food processor and blend well. Take a frying pan and place it over medium heat, add oil and allow the oil to heat up. Add salmon and sear for 3 minutes on both sides (1 and a ½ minute preside). Add walnuts mix on top. Transfer the coated salmon to your baking sheet and bake for 8 minutes. Enjoy!

Nutritional Information per Serving

Calories: 524; Total Fat: 38 g; Carbs: 5 g; Dietary Fiber: 2 g;
Protein: 39 g; Cholesterol: 101 mg; Sodium: 422 mg

DINNER - EXTREMELY REFRESHING BLUEBERRY SMOOTHIE

Yield: 2
Total Time: 5 minutes
Prep Time: 5 minutes
Cooking Time: 0 minutes

Ingredients
- 3 tablespoons of Golden Flaxseed Meal
- 1 tablespoon of Chia Seeds
- 2 cups of Unsweetened Coconut Milk
- 10 drops of Liquid Stevia
- ¼ cup of Blueberries
- 2 tablespoons of MCT Oil
- 1 and a ½ teaspoon of Banana Extract
- ¼ a teaspoon of Xanthan Gum

Instructions
Take a blender and add all of the listed ingredients. Let the whole mixture sit for a while to allow the chia to settle in. Blend for 1-2 minutes until it smooth. Serve chilled!

Nutritional Information per Serving
Calories: 132; Total Fat: 6 g; Carbs: 17 g; Dietary Fiber: 3 g; Protein: 4 g; Cholesterol: 0 mg; Sodium: 34 mg

Chapter 19: Day 16 Meals

Thank you for allowing us to expose you to the large variety of Keto Meal Prep recipes that you can enjoy, please feel free to leave us a positive review if you like what you are about to read through.

BREAKFAST - COCONUT CHIA PUDDING

Yield: 1 Servings
Total Time: 20 Minutes
Prep Time: 10 Minutes
Cook Time: 15 Minutes

Ingredients:

- Chia seeds: ¼ cup
- Full fat coconut milk: 1 cup
- Honey: ½ tablespoon
- Mango chunks: ½ cup
- Pineapple chunks: ½ cup
- Flaked coconut: 1 tablespoon

Instructions:

Take a bowl and then mix together the chia seeds, full fat coconut milk and the honey. Put the bowl in the refrigerator to set for a few hours preferably overnight until it is completely set. Take out your pudding from the refrigerator. Cut the mango and the pineapple in to small chunks and then top your pudding with these fruit chunks. Sprinkle over the flaked coconut before serving.

Nutritional Information per Serving

Calories: 206; Total Fat: 19 g; Carbs: 20.3 g; Dietary Fiber: 2.6 g;
Protein: 4.6 g; Cholesterol: 89 mg; Sodium: 928 mg

LUNCH - STIRRED CABBAGE FRY

Yield: 4
Total Time: 45 minutes
Prep Time: 15 minutes
Cooking Time: 30 minutes

Ingredients

- 1 and a 2/3 pound of green cabbage
- 5 and a 1/3 ounce of butter
- 1 and a 1/3 pound of ground beef
- 1 teaspoon of salt
- 1 teaspoon of onion powder
- ¼ teaspoon of ground black pepper
- 1 tablespoon of white wine vinegar
- 2 garlic cloves
- 3 scallions sliced up
- 1 teaspoon of chili flakes
- 1 tablespoon of fresh ginger, chopped and grated
- 1 tablespoon of sesame oil

Instructions

Shred the cabbage using a food processor. Fry your cabbage in 23 ounces of utter in a large sized frying pan and place it over medium-high heat. Add spices, vinegar and stir well for a few minutes. Transfer the cabbage to a bowl. Melt the rest of the butter and add garlic, ginger, chili flakes and sauté for a few minutes. Add ground meat and sauté for a while. Once the juices have evaporated, lower down the heat and add scallions and pepper. Top it up with sesame oil and enjoy!

Nutritional Information per Serving

Calories: 268; Total Fat: 13 g; Carbs: 9 g; Dietary Fiber: 2 g;
Protein: 29 g; Cholesterol: 83 mg; Sodium: 687 mg

DINNER - SUPREME CLOUD BREADS

Yield: 2
Total Time: 20 minutes
Prep Time: 10 minutes
Cooking Time: 10 minutes

Ingredients
Required for the Cloud Bread:
- 3 large pieces of eggs
- 3 ounce of cream cheese
- 1/8 teaspoon of tartar cream
- ¼ teaspoon of salt
- ½ teaspoon of garlic powder

Required for the filling:
- 1 tablespoon of mayonnaise
- 1 teaspoon of Sriracha
- 2 Bacon slices
- 3 ounces of Chicken
- 2 pepper jack cheese slices
- 2 grape tomatoes
- ¼ of a medium sized avocado

Instructions

Pre-heat your oven to a temperature of 300-degree Fahrenheit. Take two clean bowls and separate your 3 eggs (one for whites and one for the yolk). Add tartar cream and salt to the whites. Whip the eggs using a hand mixer until a foamy texture appears.

In the other bowl, add 3 ounce of cream cheese and beat the yolks until a nice pale-yellow texture comes. Fold the white's mixture into your yolk mixture, half at a time

Take a baking sheet and line it up with parchment paper.

Add ¼ cup of your cloud bread batter into six individual rounds. Take a spatula and gently press the cloud breads to make a square. Sprinkle a bit of garlic powder and bake for about 25 minutes. Take a medium sized skillet and add your chicken and bacon. Season with some salt and cook them until a brown texture comes. Take a small bowl and add sriracha and mayonnaise. Spread about 1/3 of the mixture on the underside of your 3 Keto breads. Add your chicken on top. Add about 2 slices of your pepper jack cheese, 2 halved grape tomatoes, 2 slices of bacon, and just 2 ounces of mashed avocado on top of your sandwich. Season with some salt and pepper and top it up with another bread. Serve!

Nutritional Information per Serving
Calories: 269; Total Fat: 17 g; Carbs: 7 g; Dietary Fiber: 2 g;
Protein: 23 g; Cholesterol: 185 mg; Sodium: 303 mg

Chapter 20: Day 17 Meals

BREAKFAST - EGG PORRIDGE
Yield: 1 Servings
Total Time: 20 Minutes
Prep Time: 5 Minutes
Cook Time: 15 Minutes

Ingredients
- Organic free eggs: 2
- Heavy cream: 1/3 cup
- No carb sweetener: 2 packages
- Grass-fed butter: 2 tablespoons
- Ground cinnamon: a pinch

Instructions
Take a whisk and whisk together the eggs, heavy cream and the no carb sweetener. Melt the grass-fed butter in to a medium frying pan and make sure that the butter does not start to burn or turn brown but it should just be melted enough. To be safe, reduce heat to low once the butter has melted. Put in the egg and cream mixture and keep on cooking and mixing until the mixture starts to get thick and starts curdling. The first signs of curdling mean the tiny grains so take off the frying pan from heat immediately. Pour the porridge in to serving bowls and it is ready now. Sprinkle over the ground cinnamon before serving!

Nutritional Information per Serving
Calories: 661; Total Fat: 64.5 g; Carbs: 2.9 g; Dietary Fiber: 3 g;
Protein: 17.3 g; Cholesterol: 53 mg; Sodium: 678 mg

LUNCH - SKIRT STEAK AND CILANTRO LIME

Yield: 2
Total Time: 55 minutes
Prep Time: 45 minutes
Cooking Time: 10 minutes

Ingredients
For the Cilantro Lime Steak Marinade:
- 1 pound of Skirt Steak
- ¼ cup of Soy Sauce
- ¼ cup of Olive Oil
- 1 medium sized lime completely juiced
- 1 teaspoon of Minced Garlic
- 1 small sized Handful Cilantro
- ¼ teaspoon of Red Pepper Flakes

For the Cilantro Paste:
- 1 teaspoon of Minced Garlic
- ½ a teaspoon of Salt
- 1 cup of lightly fresh cilantro
- ¼ cup of olive oil
- ½ a medium sized juiced lemon
- 1 medium sized deseeded Jalapeno
- ½ a teaspoon of Cumin
- ½ a teaspoon of Coriander

Instructions
Remove the outer silver skin off the skirt steak. Take a plastic bag and add cilantro lime steak marinade and mix. Add the steak and coat it. Allow it to marinade for 45 minutes in your fridge. Make the sauce by adding the paste ingredients to a food processor and pulse until blended. Take an iron skillet and place it over medium-high heat. Remove the steak form the bag and add to the pan. Sear both sides giving 2-3 minutes to each side. Serve with cilantro sauce on top and enjoy!

Nutritional Information per Serving

Calories: 230; Total Fat: 9 g; Carbs: 6 g; Dietary Fiber: 2 g; Protein:30 g; Cholesterol: 77 mg; Sodium: 470 mg

DINNER - MOUTH WATERING CHEESY BITES

Yield: 2
Total Time: 20 minutes
Prep Time: 10 minutes
Cooking Time: 10 minutes

Ingredients

- 10 ounces of Drained up Canned Tuna
- ¼ cup of mayonnaise
- 1 cubed and medium sized Avocado
- ¼ cup of Parmesan Cheese
- 1/3 cup of Almond Flour
- ½ teaspoon of Garlic Powder
- ¼ teaspoon of Onion Powder
- Salt as needed
- Pepper as needed
- ½ a cup of Coconut Oil

Instructions

Take a small sized bowl and add the listed ingredients (except avocado and coconut oil). Fold in cubed avocado to the drained tuna and mix well. Form balls using the mixture and roll the balls in almond flour. Place a skillet over medium heat and add coconut oil, allow the oil to heat up. Add balls and fry until browned. Serve and enjoy!

Nutritional Information per Serving

Calories: 401; Total Fat: 27 g; Carbs: 18 g; Dietary Fiber: 3 g;
Protein: 17 g; Cholesterol: 171 mg; Sodium: 413 mg

Chapter 21: Day 18 Meals

Breakfast - Keto pumpkin pancakes

Yield: 6 Servings
Total Time: 23 Minutes
Prep Time: 15 Minutes
Cook Time: 8 Minutes

Ingredients

- Freshly ground flax seeds: 2 ounces
- Ground hazelnuts: 2 ounces
- Egg white protein: 28 grams
- Baking powder: 1 teaspoon
- Chai masala mix: 1 tablespoon
- Vanilla extract: 1 teaspoon
- Coconut cream: 1 cup
- Eggs: 3
- Pumpkin puree: ½ cup
- Stevia drops: 4 to 5
- Swerve: 1 tablespoon
- Coconut oil for frying

Instructions

Firstly, you must mix all the dry ingredients, the ground flax seeds, ground hazelnuts, egg white protein, baking powder, chai masala mix and the vanilla extract. Now add in the coconut cream, eggs, pumpkin puree, stevia drops and the swerve. Make sure that all the ingredients are properly mixed. Heat up the coconut oil in a frying pan and pour the batter in the frying pan to fry. Flip the pancake to the other side to make sure that both sides are cooked. Repeat the procedure with the remaining batter. Sprinkle over the chai masala mix before serving.

Nutritional Information per Serving

Calories: 443; Total Fat: 35 g; Carbs: 14 g; Dietary Fiber: 7 g;
Protein: 21 g; Cholesterol: 9 mg; Sodium: 126 mg

LUNCH - ASIAN CUCUMBER SALAD

Yield: 2
Total Time: 50 minutes
Prep Time: 10 minutes
Cooking Time: 40 minutes

Ingredients
- ¾ of a large cucumber
- 1 pack of Shirataki Noodles
- 2 tablespoons of Coconut Oil
- 1 medium sized Spring Onion
- ¼ a teaspoon of Red Pepper Flakes
- 1 tablespoon of Sesame Oil
- 1 tablespoon of Rice Vinegar
- 1 teaspoon of Sesame Seeds
- Salt as needed
- Pepper as needed

Instructions
Take your Shirataki noodles and finely rinse them under cold water. Drain the excess water. Take a kitchen towel and pat them dry. Take a pan and add 2 tablespoon of coconut oil and heat up the oil over medium high heat. Add the noodles and fry for about 5-7 minutes, making sure to boil off any excess water. Remove the noodle from your pan and dry it on your kitchen towel again. Slice up your cucumbers thinly and carefully assemble them on your serving plate. Add the remaining ingredients to your serving plate and let it chill for about 30 minutes. Add the fried noodles on top of your salad and serve!

Nutritional Information per Serving
Calories: 153; Total Fat: 14 g; Carbs: 8 g; Dietary Fiber: 3 g; Protein: 1 g; Cholesterol: 0 mg; Sodium: 5 mg

DINNER - PUMPKIN CARBONARA

Yield: 3
Total Time: 20 minutes
Prep Time: 10 minutes
Cooking Time: 10 minutes

Ingredients
- 1 package of Shirataki Noodles
- 5 ounces of Pancetta
- 2 large sized Egg Yolks
- ¼ cup of heavy cream
- 1/3 cup of Parmesan Cheese
- 2 tablespoons of Butter
- 3 tablespoons of Pumpkin Puree
- ½ teaspoon of Dried Sage
- Salt as needed
- Pepper as needed

Instructions
Submerge the noodle boiling water and cook them for 2-3 minutes, dry them completely. Chop the pancetta. Take a skillet and place it over medium heat, add the pancetta. Sear until you have a crispy texture, keep them on the side. Reserve the fat,
take another pan and place it over medium heat, add butter and allow the butter to melt. Add pumpkin puree and sage. Pour heavy cream and reserve fat and mix well and remove the heat.
Take another pan and place it over medium-high heat, add the noodle and dry fry them for 5 minutes. Add parmesan cheese to the pumpkin sauce and mix. Simmer the pumpkin sauce for a few minutes until the cheese has melted. Add the pancetta and pumpkin cheese sauce to the noodle and toss well. Top with 2 egg yolks and cook for a few minutes more. Enjoy!

Nutritional Information per Serving

Calories: 250; Total Fat: 20 g; Carbs: 8 g; Dietary Fiber: 1 g;
Protein: 10 g; Cholesterol: 47 mg; Sodium: 651 mg

Chapter 22: Day 19 Meals

Thank you for allowing us to expose you to the large variety of Keto Meal Prep recipes that you can enjoy, please feel free to leave us a positive review if you like what you are about to read through.

BREAKFAST - KETO WAFFLES

Yield: 5 Servings
Total Time: 20 Minutes
Prep Time: 10 Minutes
Cook Time: 10 Minutes

Ingredients:

- Eggs, separated: 5
- Coconut flour: 4 tbsp.
- Granulated sweetener: 4 tbsp.
- Baking powder: 1 tsp
- Vanilla extract: 2 tsp
- Full fat milk: 3 tbsp.
- Melted butter: 125 grams

Instructions:

Separate the egg whites and the egg yolks and beat the egg whites until they form in to stiff peaks. In another bowl, beat the egg yolks, coconut flour, granulated sweetener and the baking powder. Now slowly and gradually pour in the melted butter carefully and mix it to make sure that you have a very smooth consistency of your batter. Now add in the full fat milk and the vanilla extract.

With the help of a rubber spatula, now very gently fold in the egg whites in the mixture. Try to keep as much as air and fluffiness that you can for better results. Preheat your waffle maker and then put in the batter on to the preheated waffle maker. Cook until your waffle has turned golden brown from both the sides. Repeat the process with the remaining batter to cook your waffles. Serve!

Nutritional Information per Serving

Calories: 280; Total Fat: 11 g; Carbs: 4.5 g; Dietary Fiber: 2 g;
Protein: 7 g; Cholesterol: 0 mg; Sodium: 50 mg

LUNCH - EXTRA DELICIOUS FRIED CAKES

Yield: 12
Total Time: 15 minutes
Prep Time: 5 minutes
Cooking Time: 10 minutes

Ingredients
- 1 can of palm hearts, drained and chopped up
- ½ a cup of vegan mayo
- 2 tablespoon of coconut flour
- 2 teaspoon of Psyllium husk fiber
- ¼ teaspoon of kelp flakes
- ¼ teaspoon of cayenne pepper
- 1 teaspoon of lemon juice
- Salt as needed
- Pepper as needed

Instructions
Take a frying pan and place it over medium-low heat. Take a mixing bowl and add all of the listed ingredients and keep mixing until you have sturdy mixture. Take the mixture and form patties. Add a bit of coconut flour over the patties if they feel a bit wet. You should have four cakes, add them one by one to pan. Cook for 5 minutes first until the bottom shows a golden texture, flip and cook for 5 minutes more. Enjoy!

Nutritional Information per Serving
Calories: 344; Total Fat: 17 g; Carbs: 27 g; Dietary Fiber: 2 g;
Protein: 4 g; Cholesterol: 0 mg; Sodium: 162 mg

DINNER - THE ULTIMATE REVERSED BACON BURGER

Yield: 2
Total Time: 25 minutes
Prep Time: 10 minutes
Cooking Time: 15 minutes

Ingredients
- 1 and a ¾ pound of ground beef
- 8 slices of Chopped up Bacon
- ¼ cup of cheddar cheese
- 2 tablespoons of chopped up Chives
- 2 teaspoons of Minced Garlic
- 2 teaspoons of Black Pepper
- 1 tablespoon of Soy Sauce
- 1 and a ¼ teaspoon of Salt
- 1 teaspoon of Onion Powder
- 1 teaspoon of Worcestershire Sauce

Instructions
Take a cast iron skillet and cook up all of your chopped bacon until a fine crispy texture has appeared. Once done, remove and place them on a kitchen towel. Drain the grease for later use. Take a large mixing bowl and toss in the ground beef, 2/3 of chopped up Bacon and the spices.

Mix the meat finely alongside the spices and form 9 patties. Put about 2 tablespoons of Bacon Fat into the cast iron and place the patties once the fat is considerably hot. Let them cook for about 4-5 minutes with batches of 3-4. Remove them, cool for 5 minutes and top it off with some extra bacon, onion or cheese

Nutritional Information per Serving
Calories: 251; Total Fat: 16 g; Carbs: 9 g; Dietary Fiber: 1 g; Protein: 17 g; Cholesterol: 73 mg; Sodium: 328 mg

Chapter 23: Day 20 Meals

BREAKFAST - LOW CARB FRENCH TOAST

Yield: 18 Servings
Total Time: 1 Hour 5 Minutes
Prep Time: 10 Minutes
Cook Time: 55 Minutes

Ingredients:
Protein bread:
- Separated eggs: 12
- Whey protein: 1 cup
- Cream cheese: 4 oz

French toast:
- Eggs: 2
- Unsweetened almond milk: ½ cup
- Vanilla extract: 1 tsp
- Cinnamon: 1 tsp

Syrup:
- Butter: ½ cup
- Swerve: ½ cup
- Unsweetened almond milk: ½ cup

Instructions:
For the bread first, preheat your oven at 325 degrees Fahrenheit. Separate the eggs and beat the egg whites until very stiff. Now very gently fold in the protein powder in to the egg whites. Now either mix the reserved egg yolks or the cream cheese in to the egg white mixture. Now grease a bread pan and place the dough in to the bread pan and put it to bake in preheated oven for 40 to 45 minutes or until it turns golden brown. Let the bread cool completely before cutting it in to slices.

For the French toast, heat coconut oil in to a skillet on a medium high heat. In a bowl, beat the eggs, unsweetened almond milk, vanilla extract and the cinnamon. Dip the prepared bread slices in to the mixture and then in the skillet to fry. Cook until your French toast turns golden brown from both the sides. Repeat this process with the remaining bread slices.

For the sauce to be served with the French toast, heat butter in a sauce pan and melt it. Wait for the butter to turn golden brown. When the butter turns golden brown, add in the swerve and keep on mixing it. Immediately after you put in the swerve, add in the unsweetened almond milk and keep stirring until your sauce reaches the consistency that you desire. Pour the sauce in to a mason jar and let it cool completely before using it.

Nutritional Information per Serving
Calories: 370; Total Fat: 20 g; Carbs: 5 g; Dietary Fiber: 1 g;
Protein: 6.3 g; Cholesterol: 30 mg; Sodium: 512 mg

LUNCH - SPIRALIZED ZUCCHINI SALAD FROM ASIA

Yield: 2
Total Time: 10 minutes
Prep Time: 10 minutes
Cooking Time: 0 minutes

Ingredients
- 1 thinly spiralized medium zucchini
- 1 pound of shredded cabbage
- 1 cup of sunflower seeds
- 1 cup of sliced almonds
- ¾ cup of avocado oil
- 1/3 cup of white vinegar
- 1 teaspoon of stevia

Instructions
Cut the spiralized zucchini into small portions using a kitchen knife. Take a large sized bowl and add sunflower seeds, almonds and cabbage. Stir in zucchini. Take a small sized bowl and add olive oil, vinegar and stevia. Pour the dressing on top of the veggies and stir. Chill for 2 hours and serve!

Nutritional Information per Serving
Calories: 318; Total Fat: 2 g; Carbs: 6.8 g; Dietary Fiber: 1 g;
Protein: 13 g; Cholesterol: 0 mg; Sodium: 35 mg

DINNER - HAM STROMBOLI

Yield: 4
Total Time: 26 minutes
Prep Time: 6 minutes
Cooking Time: 20 minutes

Ingredients
- 1 and a quarter cup of shredded mozzarella cheese
- 4 tablespoons of almond flour
- 3 tablespoon of coconut flour
- 1 large sized egg
- 1 teaspoon of Italian seasoning
- 14 ounces of Ham
- 3 and a half ounces of Cheddar Cheese
- Salt as required
- Pepper as required

Instructions
Pre-heat your oven to a temperature of 400-degree Fahrenheit and melt up your mozzarella cheese in a microwave oven. Take mixing a bowl and toss in the coconut flour, almond flour and seasoning and mix them properly. Then pour in the melted mozzarella cheese and keep mixing. After a minute, the cheese will be cooled down and here toss in your egg and mix everything again. Once combined, take a fine parchment paper and on a flat surface transfer the mixture. Take a rolling pin to flat it out evenly.

Take a pizza cutter and cut diagonal lines in the dough from the starting from the edges going all the way to the center. Make sure that you leave about 4 inches wide rows of the dough untouched in between. Between the diagonal layers, fill it up with ham and cheddar. Once done, life on section of the dough and roll it on top of another. Completely covering the filling. Finally, bake it for about 15-20 minutes and serve when a nice golden-brown texture has appeared

Nutritional Information per Serving *Calories: 190; Total Fat: 7 g; Carbs: 21 g; Dietary Fiber: 2 g; Protein: 11 g; Cholesterol: 48 mg; Sodium: 580 mg*

Chapter 24: Day 21 Meals

BREAKFAST - BAKED SPICE GRANOLA

Yield: 4 Servings
Total Time: 1 Hour 45 Minutes
Prep Time: 15 Minutes
Cook Time: 1 Hour 30 Minutes

Ingredients:
- Chopped pecans: 1 cup
- Chopped walnuts: ½ cup
- Slivered almonds: ½ cup
- Flaked coconut: ½ cup
- Almond meal: ½ cup
- Ground chia seeds: ½ cup
- Pumpkin seeds: ¼ cup
- Sunflower seeds: ¼ cup
- Melted butter: ¼ cup
- Stevia: ½ cup
- Honey: 1 teaspoon
- Cinnamon: 1 teaspoon
- Vanilla extract: 1 teaspoon
- Nutmeg: ½ teaspoon
- Salt: ½ teaspoon
- Water: ¼ cup

Instructions:
Preheat your oven at 250 degrees Fahrenheit. In a bowl, mix the chopped pecans, chopped walnuts, slivered almonds, flaked coconut, almond meal, ground chia seeds, pumpkin seeds, sunflower seeds, melted butter, sweetener, honey, cinnamon, vanilla extract, salt and the water. Mix all the

ingredients properly so that they are mixed well. Grease a baking tray and place a parchment paper on it. Put your mixed mixture on to the parchment paper and put another parchment paper on to the granola mixture. With the help of a rolling pin, roll out the granola to firm it and make it even. Discard the upper parchment paper and put the baking tray in the preheated oven to bake for 60 to 90 minutes or until golden. Remove it from the oven and then allow it to cool completely before breaking in to pieces and eating.

Nutritional Information per Serving

Calories: 466; Total Fat: 12 g; Carbs: 15.23 g; Dietary Fiber: 12.24 g;
Protein: 20.29 g; Cholesterol: 0 mg; Sodium: 35 mg

LUNCH - VEGETABLE CASSEROLE

Yield: 6
Total Time: 40 minutes
Prep Time: 10 minutes
Cooking Time: 30 minutes

Ingredients

- 1 pound of pork sausage
- 2 cups of diced up zucchini
- 2 cups of shredded green cabbage
- ½ a cup of diced up onion
- 3 pieces of large eggs
- ½ a cup of mayonnaise
- 2 teaspoons of yellow mustard
- 1 teaspoon of dried ground sage
- 1 and a ½ cup of shredded and divided cheddar cheese
- Cayenne pepper as required

Instructions:

Prepare your oven by pre-heating to a temperature of 375-degree Fahrenheit. Take your casserole dish and grease it up. Take a large sized skillet and place it over medium heat. Add sausages and cook them until they have a brown texture. Add your zucchini, cabbages and onion to the same skillet and cook all of them until they are nice and tender.

Remove the heat carefully and spoon the whole mixture into your greased casserole. Take a mixing bowl and add eggs, sage, mayonnaise and pepper and whisk everything well until a smooth mixture forms. Add 1 cup of your cheese to the egg mix. Add the cheese to your casserole dish. Add the egg mix to your casserole dish. Transfer the casserole to your oven and bake for about 30 minutes. Remove it from your oven and serve!

Nutritional Information per Serving

Calories: 272; Total Fat: 14 g; Carbs: 20 g; Dietary Fiber: 1 g;
Protein: 12 g; Cholesterol: 40 mg; Sodium: 283 mg

DINNER - APPLE FLATBREAD

Yield: 8
Total Time: 35 minutes
Prep Time: 15 minutes
Cooking Time: 20 minutes

Ingredients
Ingredients required for the crust:
- 2 cups of grated partially skimmed mozzarella cheese
- ¾ cup of almond flour
- 2 tablespoon of sea salt
- 1/8 teaspoon of dried thyme

Ingredients needed for the topping:
- 2 cups of grated Mexican cheese
- ½ of a small onion sliced into thin portions
- ¼ of a medium sized apple. Seeded and cored with the skin intact
- 4 ounce of low carb ham sliced into chunks
- 1/8 teaspoon of dried thyme
- Salt as required
- Pepper as required

Instructions

Preheat your oven to a temperature of 425-degree Fahrenheit. Next, two about two pieces of parchment paper which should be about 2 inches large than a 12-inch pan pizza. Prepare a nice double boiler. Take a sauce pot and fill it up with just enough water and bring the water to simmer. Once brought to simmer, low down the heat.

Take the mixing bowl prepared for the double boiler and add in the cream cheese, mozzarella cheese, almond flour, salt and thyme. Gently place the bowl over the simmer pot and keep stirring it continuously while being careful of the steam. Once the cheese has melted down and ingredients are combined, pour down the mixture to one of the previously prepared parchment paper and knead it for a few minutes.

Roll up the whole dough into a ball and place it on the center of the paper. Gently keep patting it until a nice circular shape has appeared. Cover it with the other parchment paper. Take a rolling pin and keep rolling the dough until it has a nice 12-inch radius.
Place the prepared dough on a pizza pan and take a fork to drill holes all over. Bake it for about 8 minutes.

Once a golden texture has appeared, lower down the heat to 350-degree Fahrenheit. Sprinkle about ¼ cup of the cheese. Finely place the sliced onion, apple and ham. Bake it again for 5-7 minutes until the cheese has melted and browned. Place it on a cooling rack and let it cool for about 3 minutes before cutting into 8 individual slices.

Nutritional Information per Serving
Calories: 277; Total Fat: 12 g; Carbs: 25 g; Dietary Fiber: 1 g;
Protein: 10 g; Cholesterol: 18 mg; Sodium: 347 mg

Chapter 25: Day 22 Meals

Thank you for allowing us to expose you to the large variety of Keto Meal Prep recipes that you can enjoy, please feel free to leave us a positive review if you like what you are about to read through.

BREAKFAST - LOW CARB GRANOLA

Yield: 48 Servings
Total Time: 35 Minutes
Prep Time: 10 Minutes
Cook Time: 25 Minutes

Ingredients:

- Chopped pecans: 2 cups
- Chopped walnuts: ½ cup
- Slivered almonds: ½ cup
- Sunflower seeds: 1 cup
- Egg white protein: 1 ¾ cup
- Sesame seeds: ½ cup
- Coconut oil: 1 ¼ cup
- Swerve: ½ cup
- Stevia glycerite: 1 teaspoon
- Ground cinnamon: 1 teaspoon
- Celtic sea salt: ½ teaspoon

Instructions:

Preheat your oven at 300 degrees Fahrenheit. In a bowl, mix together the chopped pecans, chopped walnuts, slivered almonds, sunflower seeds, egg white protein, sesame seeds, swerve, stevia glycerite, ground cinnamon and the Celtic sea salt. Melt the coconut oil and pour over the mixture and mix well. Place the granola on to a baking sheet and put the tray to bake in the preheated oven for 20 to 25 minutes or until it turns golden brown. Remove from the oven and let it cool completely before breaking in to pieces. Serve your granola bars with unsweetened almond milk or vanilla milk.

Nutritional Information per Serving

Calories: 130; Total Fat: 2 g; Carbs: 22 g; Dietary Fiber: 2 g;
Protein: 4 g; Cholesterol: 0 mg; Sodium: 35 mg

LUNCH - NO FUSS PUMPKIN FUDGE

Yield: 25
Total Time: 135 minutes
Prep Time: 15 minutes
Cooking Time: 120 minutes

Ingredients

- 1 and a ¾ cup of coconut butter
- 1 cup of pumpkin puree
- 1 teaspoon of ground cinnamon
- ¼ teaspoon of ground nutmeg
- 1 tablespoon of coconut oil

Instructions

Take an 8x8 inch square baking pan and line it up with aluminum foil.

Take a spoon and scoop out coconut butter and add to the heated pan. Allow the butter to melt. Keep stirring well and remove the heat once melted and add spices and pumpkin. Keep stirring until you have a grainy texture. Add coconut oil and mix well

Scoop the mixture into your baking pan and distribute it evenly. Place a wax paper on top of the mixture and press it gently to even the top. Chill for 1-2 hours. Cut in slices and enjoy

Nutritional Information per Serving

Calories: 358; Total Fat: 17 g; Carbs: 14 g; Dietary Fiber: 2 g;
Protein: 2 g; Cholesterol: 24 mg; Sodium: 35 mg

DINNER - EARLY MORNING BROWNIE MUFFIN

Yield: 5
Total Time: 45 minutes
Prep Time: 10 minutes
Cooking Time: 35 minutes

Ingredients

- 1 cup of Golden Flaxseed Meal
- ¼ cup of cocoa powder
- 1 tablespoon of Cinnamon
- ½ tablespoon of Baking Powder
- ½ a teaspoon of Salt
- 1 piece of large egg
- 2 tablespoons of Coconut Oil
- ¼ cup of Sugar free Caramel Syrup
- ½ a cup of Pumpkin Puree
- 1 teaspoon of Vanilla Extract
- 1 teaspoon of Apple Cider Vinegar
- ¼ cup of Silvered Almond

Instructions

Preheat your oven to a temperature of 350-degree Fahrenheit. Take a mixing bowl and add all of the listed ingredients. Mix well. Take your muffin tins and line them up with muffin liners. Scoop up the batter to each of your muffin tins, making sure that they are 1/4th full. Place the tins in your oven and bake for 15 minutes. Serve warm!

Nutritional Information per Serving

Calories: 197; Total Fat: 7 g; Carbs: 25 g; Dietary Fiber: 1 g; Protein: 3 g; Cholesterol: 0 mg; Sodium: 357 mg

Chapter 26: Day 23 Meals

BREAKFAST - THE BEST KETO BREAKFAST

Yield: 2 Servings
Total Time: 8 Minutes
Prep Time: 2 Minutes
Cook Time: 6 Minutes

Ingredients:
- Pastured bacon strips: 4
- Peeled avocado: 1
- Organic eggs: 2
- Sea salt: ¼ teaspoon

Instructions:
Remove the seed from the avocado and put the avocado and the bacon strips on a frying pan on medium flame. After 2 to 3 minutes flip the avocado and the bacon strip to the other side to cook properly. Remove the avocado and the bacon strips and set aside. Break the eggs in to the frying pan and fry for 2 to 3 minutes and then flip to the other side when cooked. Place the eggs in to the plate along with the bacon strips and the avocado. Serve!

Nutritional Information per Serving
Calories: 313; Total Fat: 26 g; Carbs: 15 g; Dietary Fiber: 6 g;
Protein: 13 g; Cholesterol: 87 mg; Sodium: 462 mg

LUNCH - HEALTHY SAUSAGE AND PEPPER SOUP

Yield: 2
Total Time: 55 minutes
Prep Time: 10 minutes
Cooking Time: 45 minutes

Ingredients

- 32 ounces of Pork Sausages
- 1 tablespoon of Olive Oil
- 10 ounces of Raw Spinach
- 1 medium sized Green Bell Pepper
- 1 can of jalapenos with tomatoes
- 4 cup of beef stock
- 1 tablespoon of chili powder
- 1 tablespoon of cumin
- 1 teaspoon of Garlic Powder
- 1 teaspoon of Italian Seasoning
- ¾ teaspoon of Salt

Instructions

Take a large sized pot and place it over medium heat. Add olive oil and allow the oil to heat up. Add sausage and cook until seared all around. Slice the green pepper into small pieces and add them to the pot. Season with salt and pepper. Add tomatoes and jalapenos and stir. Add spinach on top and cover with lid, wait until the spinach has wilted. Add the rest of the spices and broth. Cook for 30 minutes over medium-low heat. Remove the lid and simmer for 15 minutes over low heat. Serve and enjoy!

Nutritional Information per Serving

Calories: 725; Total Fat: 56 g; Carbs: 32 g; Dietary Fiber: 3 g;
Protein: 26 g; Cholesterol: 108 mg; Sodium: 1419 mg

DINNER - CHARRED UP GARLIC ARTICHOKES

Yield: 4
Total Time: 35 minutes
Prep Time: 5 minutes
Cooking Time: 30 minutes

Ingredients

- 2 large sized artichokes
- 1 quartered lemon
- ¾ cup of olive oil
- 4 chopped up garlic cloves
- 1 teaspoon of salt
- ½ a teaspoon of ground black pepper

Instructions

Take a large sized bowl and add water. Squeeze lemon juice in the water. Trim the top of the artichokes and cut them half-lengthwise. Bring the water to a boil and add the artichokes, allow them to cook for 15 minutes. While they are being cooked, pre-heat your grill to medium-high. Once the chokes are cooked, drain them and squeeze the rest of the lemon wedges into a medium sized bowl.

Stir in garlic and olive oil. Season with pepper and salt. Brush the chokes with the coating of garlic dip and place them on the pre-heated grill. Grill for 10 minutes, makings sure to keep basting it from time to time. Serve the grilled artichokes with the rest of the dips

Nutritional Information per Serving

Calories: 237; Total Fat: 19 g; Carbs: 16 g; Dietary Fiber: 2 g;
Protein: 5 g; Cholesterol: 32 mg; Sodium: 849 mg

Chapter 27: Day 24 Meals

Thank you for allowing us to expose you to the large variety of Keto Meal Prep recipes that you can enjoy, please feel free to leave us a positive review if you like what you are about to read through.

BREAKFAST - KETO BREAKFAST

Yield: 1 Servings
Total Time: 20 Minutes
Prep Time: 10 Minutes
Cook Time: 10 Minutes

Ingredients:

- Medium size zucchini: 1
- Bacon slices: 2
- Onion: ½
- Coconut oil: 1 tablespoon
- Chopped parsley: 1 tablespoon
- Salt: ¼ teaspoon
- Egg: 1

Instructions:

Firstly, chop the onion in to small pieces and then cut the bacon strips in to small pieces as well. Cook the onion and the bacon pieces in to a frying pan until lightly browned. Cut the zucchini in to small cubes. Now add the zucchini pieces in to the frying pan and cook for few more minutes. Remove from the heat and then add in the chopped parsley. In a separate frying pan, fry the egg carefully and season it will salt. Serve your plate by putting on the zucchini, onion and bacon mixture and top it with the fried egg. Serve!

Nutritional Information per Serving

Calories: 423; Total Fat: 35.5 g; Carbs: 8 g; Dietary Fiber: 2.5 g;
Protein: 17.4 g; Cholesterol: 0 mg; Sodium: 698 mg

LUNCH - COOL COLLARD GREENS

Yield: 6
Total Time: 70 minutes
Prep Time: 10 minutes
Cooking Time: 60 minutes

Ingredients
- 1 tablespoon of olive oil
- 3 slices of bacon
- 1 chopped up large onion
- 2 minced garlic cloves
- 1 teaspoon of salt
- 3 cups of chicken broth
- 1 pinch of red pepper flakes
- 1 pound of fresh collard greens cut up into 2-inch pieces

Instructions
Take a large sized pan and place it over medium high heat. Add oil and allow the oil to heat up. Add bacon and cook for a while until crispy, crumble the bacon and add the crumbled bacon back to the pan. Add onion and cook for 5 minutes. Add garlic and cook until a nice fragrance comes. Add collard greens and keep frying until thyme wilt.
Add chicken broth, season with salt and pepper flakes. Enjoy!

Nutritional Information per Serving
Calories: 351; Total Fat: 24 g; Carbs: 17 g; Dietary Fiber: 3 g;
Protein: 17 g; Cholesterol: 55 mg; Sodium: 725 mg

DINNER - WATERMELON AND ICE SALAD

Yield: 10
Total Time: 15 minutes
Prep Time: 15 minutes
Cooking Time: 0 minutes

Ingredients
- 3 cups of chopped up watermelon
- ½ a cup of chopped up green bell pepper
- 2 tablespoon of lime juice
- 2 tablespoons of chopped fresh cilantro
- 1 tablespoon of chopped green onions
- 1 tablespoon of chopped jalapeno
- ½ a teaspoon of garlic salt

Instructions
Take a large sized bowl and add lime juice, watermelon, cilantro, green bell pepper, green onion, garlic salt, jalapeno and green onion. Give it a mix and toss well. Serve chilled!

Nutritional Information per Serving
Calories: 175; Total Fat: 7 g; Carbs: 23 g; Dietary Fiber: 2 g; Protein: 7 g; Cholesterol: 14 mg; Sodium: 142 mg

Chapter 28: Day 25 Meals

BREAKFAST - KETO GREEN BUTTERED EGGS

Yield: 2 Servings
Total Time: 14 Minutes
Prep Time: 5 Minutes
Cook Time: 9 Minutes

Ingredients

- Organic butter: 2 tablespoons
- Coconut oil: 1 tablespoon
- Garlic cloves: 2
- Fresh thyme leaves: 1 teaspoon
- Chopped cilantro: ½ cup
- Chopped parsley: ½ cup
- Organic eggs: 4
- Ground cumin: ¼ teaspoon
- Ground cayenne: ¼ teaspoon
- Sea salt: ½ teaspoon

Instructions

Take a skillet, and melt in the coconut oil and the butter. Chop the garlic clove and fry in the skillet until it turns golden brown. Now add in the fresh thyme leaves and be careful not to burn the garlic. Now add in the chopped cilantro and the parsley and cook for 2 to 3 minutes until brown and crisp. Now add in the eggs to the skillet and make sure that you do not break the egg yolk. Season with ground cumin and the ground cayenne. Cover the skillet with a lid and let cook for a while at least 5 to 6 minutes. Serve immediately!

Nutritional Information per Serving

Calories: 311; Total Fat: 27.5 g; Carbs: 8 g; Dietary Fiber: 1 g;
Protein: 12.8 g; Cholesterol: 20 mg; Sodium: 285 mg

LUNCH - THE PERFECT MINI PANCAKE

Yield: 2
Total Time: 15 minutes
Prep Time: 5 minutes
Cooking Time: 10 minutes

Ingredients

For the Peanut Filling:
- 1.8 ounce of Fresh Shelled Peanuts
- ½ a teaspoon of Stevia
- Salt as needed

For the Condensed Milk:
- ¼ cup of Heavy cream
- 2 drops of Liquid Sucralose

For the Apam Balik:
- ½ a cup of Almond Flour
- ½ a teaspoon of Bicarbonate Soda
- ½ a teaspoon of Baking Powder
- 1/8 teaspoon of Salt
- ¼ cup of Almond Milk
- 1 large sized Egg
- 5 drops of Liquid Sucralose
- ½ a teaspoon of Vanilla Extract
- ¼ teaspoon of coconut oil
- 1 tablespoon of Unsalted Butter

Instructions

Take a large sized skillet and place it over medium heat. Once heated, add peanuts and toast them. Grind the peanuts with stevia and season with salt. Take a pot and place it over medium heat. Add heavy cream, sucralose to the pot and keep mixing until you have a thick texture. Take another mixing bowl and add salt, almond flour, baking soda and baking powder. Mix well.

Add almond milk, egg, sucralose, vanilla extract to the flour mixture. Take a pan and place it over medium heat. Add coconut oil and allow the oil to heat up

Pour the batter to the pan and cook for 1 minute. Add ground peanuts and cover the pan. Cook until you have a brown texture. Remove and serve! If you have any left –over batter, repeat the process

Nutritional Information per Serving
Calories: 137; Total Fat: 5 g; Carbs: 18 g; Dietary Fiber: 1 g; Protein: 6 g; Cholesterol: 30 mg; Sodium: 138 mg

Dinner - Mung Bean "Faux" Meatballs

Yield: 4
Total Time: 45 minutes
Prep Time: 20 minutes
Cooking Time: 25 minutes

Ingredients

- 1 tablespoon of ground flaxseed
- 1 and a ½ cups of cooked mung beans
- ½ a cup of black ripe olives chopped up
- ½ a cup of finely chopped onions
- 2 tablespoons of sun-dried tomatoes chopped up
- ¼ cup of chopped fresh parsley
- 1 minced garlic clove
- 1 teaspoon of dried oregano
- ¼ teaspoon of red chili flakes
- ¼ teaspoon of freshly ground black pepper
- ¼ teaspoon of salt
- 2 tablespoon of sugar free tomato sauce

Instructions

Pre-heat your oven to 350-degree Fahrenheit. Take a small sized bowl and add flaxseed and 3 tablespoons of water. Keep it on the side for 10 minutes. Take a medium sized bowl and add mung beans, mash with potato masher. Pulse the mixture in food processor until you have a smooth texture. Add olives, garlic, onion, tomato sauce; sun dried tomatoes, parsley, spices and pulse. Add flax and pulse.

Roll up your bean mixture into 1 and a ½ inch balls and transfer them evenly on a paper lined up baking sheet. Cook for about 20 minutes, making sure to give them a flip. Cook for another 10 minutes after the flip. Once the balls are browned, serve and enjoy!

Nutritional Information per Serving *Calories: 279; Total Fat: 16 g; Carbs: 18 g; Dietary Fiber: 1 g; Protein: 17 g; Cholesterol: 42 mg; Sodium: 602 mg*

Chapter 29: Day 26 Meals

Breakfast - Cheddar and chive souffles

Yield: 8 Servings
Total Time: 40 Minutes
Prep Time: 15 Minutes
Cook Time: 25 Minutes

Ingredients:
- Almond flour: ½ cup
- Salt: 1 teaspoon
- Ground mustard: 1 teaspoon
- Black pepper: ½ teaspoon
- Xanthan gum: ½ teaspoon
- Cayenne pepper: ¼ teaspoon
- Heavy cream: ¾ cup
- Shredded cheddar cheese: 2 cups
- Chopped chives: ¼ cup
- Eggs: 6
- Cream of tartar: ¼ teaspoon
- Salt: a pinch

Instructions:
Preheat your oven at 350 degrees Fahrenheit. Grease 8 round ramekins. In a bowl, mix together the almond flour, salt, ground mustard, black pepper, xanthan gum, cayenne pepper, heavy cream and the shredded cheddar cheese. Now mix in the chopped fresh chives. Mix all the ingredients properly. Separate the egg yolks and the egg whites and mix in the egg yolks in the mixture.

In another bowl, beat the egg whites and the cream of tartar until stiff peaks form. Add a pinch of salt. Fold the egg whites in to the egg yolk mixture to incorporate well. Divide this mixture in to the greased ramekins and put them to bake in preheated oven for 20 to 25 minutes or until the soufflé rises and turns golden brown. Serve immediately!

Nutritional Information per Serving

Calories: 288; Total Fat: 16 g; Carbs: 3.32 g; Dietary Fiber: 1 g;
Protein: 14 g; Cholesterol: 23 mg; Sodium: 724 mg

LUNCH - LIGHTLY SAUTÉED MUSHROOMS

Yield: 2
Total Time: 30 minutes
Prep Time: 10 minutes
Cooking Time: 20 minutes

Ingredients

- 2 tablespoons of butter
- 1 tablespoon of olive oil
- 1 and a ½ pound of gourmet mushroom
- 4 diced up garlic cloves
- 1/3 cup of dry white wine
- Salt as needed

Instructions

Take a heavy pan and place it over medium heat, allow it to heat up. Pour oil and ½ of butter. Wait until smoking hot and add mushrooms. Keep stirring the mushroom until browned. Add another ½ of your butter and garlic. Keep stirring to ensure that they are not burned, add white wine and allow it to cook. Keep cooking until the liquid has been fully absorbed, season with salt and serve!

Nutritional Information per Serving

Calories: 106; Total Fat: 5 g; Carbs: 13 g; Dietary Fiber: 2 g;
Protein: 5 g; Cholesterol: 0 mg; Sodium: 648 mg

DINNER - EXTREME ZUCCHINI SAUTÉ

Yield: 6
Total Time: 30 minutes
Prep Time: 15 minutes
Cooking Time: 15 minutes

Ingredients

- 1 tablespoon of olive oil
- ½ of a diced red onion
- Salt as needed
- Pepper as needed
- 4 halved and sliced Zucchini
- ½ a pound of fresh sliced mushrooms
- 1 diced tomato
- 1 minced clove of garlic
- 1 teaspoon of Italian seasoning

Instructions

Take a large sized skillet and place it over medium heat. Add onion and saute for 2 minutes. Season with some salt and pepper. Add zucchini to the skillet. Once the zucchini is tender, add garlic and Italian seasoning alongside the tomatoes. Cook well and enjoy!

Nutritional Information per Serving

Calories: 230; Total Fat: 22 g; Carbs: 4 g; Dietary Fiber: 1 g;
Protein: 5 g; Cholesterol: 17 mg; Sodium: 176 mg

Chapter 30: Day 27 Meals

BREAKFAST - AVOCADO AND SALMON LOW CARB BREAKFAST

Yield: 1 Servings
Total Time: 20 Minutes
Prep Time: 5 Minutes
Cook Time: 15 Minutes

Ingredients:
- Ripe avocado: 1
- Smoked salmon: 60 grams
- Soft goat cheese: 30 grams
- Organic extra virgin olive oil: 2 tablespoons
- Lemon juice of 1
- Celtic sea salt: a pinch

Instructions:
Cut the avocado in to half and remove the seed from within the avocado. Take a blender and add the smoked salmon, soft goat cheese, organic extra virgin olive oil, lemon juice and the Celtic sea salt pinch and blend the ingredients until they are coarsely chopped.

Put this blended cream in to the avocado where you removed the avocado seed. Serve immediately. An alternative to this way is to chop both the avocado and the salmon and mix both. Now add in the goat cheese and the rest of the ingredients and then blend them together and serve.

Nutritional Information per Serving
Calories: 525; Total Fat: 48 g; Carbs: 4 g; Dietary Fiber: 13 g;
Protein: 19 g; Cholesterol: 43 mg; Sodium: 126 mg

LUNCH - DELICIOUS LEMON BROCCOLI

Yield: 6
Total Time: 25 minutes
Prep Time: 10 minutes
Cooking Time: 15 minutes

Ingredients

- 2 heads of broccoli separated into florets
- 2 teaspoon of extra virgin olive oil
- 1 teaspoon of sea salt
- ½ a teaspoon of ground black pepper
- 1 minced garlic clove
- ½ a teaspoon of lemon juice

Instructions

Pre-heat your oven to 400-degree Fahrenheit. Take a large sized bowl and add broccoli florets alongside some extra virgin olive oil, sea salt, pepper, garlic.
Spread the broccoli mix in a single layer on a baking sheet and bake for 15-20 minutes until the florets are fork tender. Squeeze lemon juice over them and serve!

Nutritional Information per Serving

Calories: 130; Total Fat: 10 g; Carbs: 6 g; Dietary Fiber: 3 g;
Protein: 6 g; Cholesterol: 10 mg; Sodium: 305 mg

DINNER - YUMMY MAC AND CHEESE WITH A HEALTHY "VEGAN" SAUCE

Yield: 6
Total Time: 55 minutes
Prep Time: 5 minutes
Cooking Time: 50 minutes

Ingredients
For Vegan Cheese Sauce
- 1 cup of hemp sees
- ½ a cup of nutritional yeast
- ¼ cup of chopped red pepper
- 1 teaspoon of salt
- ½ a teaspoon of onion powder
- ½ a teaspoon of garlic powder
- ½ -1 cup of water

For Macaroni
- 1 pack of Shirataki macaroni
- ¼ cup of the above prepared sauce

Instructions
Pre-heat your oven to 350-degree Fahrenheit. Take a blender and add the sauce ingredients and mi until smooth. You should have a queso like consistency. Rinse and drain your macaroni. Add the noodles and the sauce in small sized baking dish and bake for about 45 minutes. Enjoy!

Nutritional Information per Serving
Calories: 320; Total Fat: 3 g; Carbs: 35 g; Dietary Fiber: 1 g;
Protein: 21 g; Cholesterol: 0 mg; Sodium: 321 mg

Chapter 31: Day 28 Meals

Thank you for allowing us to expose you to the large variety of Keto Meal Prep recipes that you can enjoy, please feel free to leave us a positive review if you like what you are about to read through.

Breakfast - Egg breakfast biscuit

Yield: 1 Servings
Total Time: 20 Minutes
Prep Time: 5 Minutes
Cook Time: 15 Minutes

Ingredients:

- Softened cream cheese: 1 ounce
- Grated parmesan cheese: 2 tablespoons
- Whole psyllium husks: ½ teaspoon
- Baking powder: 1/8 teaspoon
- Apple cider vinegar: ½ teaspoon
- Granulated garlic: 1
- Kosher salt: a pinch
- Black pepper: a pinch
- Eggs: 2
- Extra virgin olive oil: 2 tablespoons
- Deluxe American cheese: ½ slice

Instructions:

Separate one of the 2 eggs. Soften the cream cheese and add in the parmesan cheese, psyllium, baking powder and the apple cider vinegar. Now add in the granulated garlic, kosher salt and the egg white from one egg. Mix all the ingredients well and blend them. Grease a few ramekins with olive oil and divide the mixture between the ramekins and put them to microwave for 30 to 45 seconds each one at a time.

The centers should be done. Heat olive oil in the skillet and put in the egg biscuit and cook until they turn golden brown from both sides. Remove it from the heat and then put on the biscuit the slice of the deluxe American cheese and let it melt. In the meanwhile, fry another egg along with the reserved egg yolk. Put the fried egg on the biscuit and top the egg with another piece of the biscuit. Serve immediately.

Nutritional Information per Serving

Calories: 572; Total Fat: 11 g; Carbs: 1 g; Dietary Fiber: 1 g; Protein:2 1 g; Cholesterol: 60 mg; Sodium: 55 mg

LUNCH - CRISPY SESAME BREAD

Yield: 20
Total Time: 85 minutes
Prep Time: 10 minutes
Cooking Time: 75 minutes

Ingredients

- 1 cup of sesame seeds
- 1 cup of sunflower seeds
- 1 cup of flaxseeds
- ½ a cup of hulled hemp seeds
- 3 tablespoon of Psyllium husk
- 1 teaspoon of salt
- 1 teaspoon of baking powder
- 2 cups of water

Instructions

Pre-heat your oven to 350-degree Fahrenheit. Take a blender and add seeds, baking powder, Psyllium husk and salt. Blend until you have a sandy texture. Stir in water and keep mixing until you have a nice batter. Let the batter rest for about 10 minutes until you have a dough like thick mixture. Transfer the dough onto a cookie sheet lined with parchment paper. Spread it evenly until you have a thickness of ¼ inch. Bake for 75 minutes. Remove and cut up into 20 pieces. Cool and enjoy!

Nutritional Information per Serving

Calories: 175; Total Fat: 6 g; Carbs: 26 g; Dietary Fiber: 2 g;
Protein: 6 g; Cholesterol: 0 mg; Sodium: 151 mg

DINNER - SIMPLE CLEANSING AVOCADO SALAD AND CILANTRO

Yield: 6
Total Time: 10 minutes
Prep Time: 10 minutes
Cooking Time: 0 minutes

Ingredients

- 2 avocados – peeled, pitted and diced
- 1 chopped up sweet onion
- 1 green bell pepper (chopped up)
- 1 large sized chopped up ripe tomato
- ¼ cup of chopped up fresh cilantro
- ½ of a juiced lime
- Salt as needed
- Pepper as needed

Instructions

Take a medium sized bowl and add onions, avocados, tomato, bell pepper, lime juice and cilantro. Mix well and coat everything well with the juice. Season with a bit of salt and pepper. Serve chilled!

Nutritional Information per Serving

Calories: 441; Total Fat: 33 g; Carbs: 21 g; Dietary Fiber: 2 g;
Protein: 12 g; Cholesterol: 0 mg; Sodium: 243 mg

Chapter 32: Day 29 Meals

BREAKFAST - SWISS CHARD AND RICOTTA PIE

Yield: 6 Servings
Total Time: 40 Minutes
Prep Time: 10 Minutes
Cook Time: 30 Minutes

Ingredients
- Olive oil: 1 tablespoon
- Chopped onion: ½ cup
- Garlic clove: 1
- Chopped swiss chard: 8 cups
- Whole milk ricotta cheese: 2 cups
- Eggs: 3
- Shredded mozzarella: 1 cup
- Shredded parmesan: ¼ cup
- Ground nutmeg: 1/8 teaspoon
- Salt: a pinch
- Pepper: a pinch
- Mild sausage: 1 lb.

Instructions
Heat olive oil in a pan and fry the chopped onion and the garlic clove which is minced. Now add in the chopped swiss chard and fry until the leaves are wilted and the stems have become tender. Now add in the ground nutmeg and season with salt and pepper. Set it aside. In another large bowl, beat the eggs and then add in the whole milk ricotta cheese, parmesan cheese and the mozzarella cheese. Now add in the fried swiss chard mixture. If you wish to make a large pie you need to roll out your sausage and press it in to a pie tart and then put in the filling which you have prepared. Preheat your oven at 350 degrees Fahrenheit and put your pie to bake in

for 25 to 30 minutes. You can add in more cheese if you wish to.

Nutritional Information per Serving
Calories: 344; Total Fat: 27 g; Carbs: 4 g; Dietary Fiber: 15 g;
Protein: 23 g; Cholesterol: 50 mg; Sodium: 528 mg

LUNCH - BLISTERED BEANS AND ALMONDS

Yield: 4
Total Time: 30 minutes
Prep Time: 10 minutes
Cooking Time: 20 minutes

Ingredients
- 1 pound of fresh green beans with their ends trimmed up
- 1 and a ½ tablespoon of olive oil
- ¼ teaspoon of salt
- 1 and a ½ tablespoon of minced up fresh dill
- Juice of just one lemon
- ¼ cup of crushed up almonds
- Flaky sea salt for finishing

Instructions
Pre-heat your oven to 400-degree Fahrenheit. Take a bowl and mix green beans with olive oil. Season with a bit of salt. Spread the mixture in a single layer on a large sized sheet pan. Roast in your oven for 10 minutes and stir well, roast for 8-10 minutes more. Remove from oven and keep stirring while gently adding lemon juice and dill. Top with some crushed almonds and salt, enjoy!

Nutritional Information per Serving
Calories: 126; Total Fat: 8 g; Carbs: 13 g; Dietary Fiber: 1 g;
Protein: 4 g; Cholesterol: 0 mg; Sodium: 501 mg

DINNER - SUBTLE ROASTED PEPPER SOUP

Yield: 4
Total Time: 35 minutes
Prep Time: 5 minutes
Cooking Time: 30 minutes

Ingredients

- 2 tablespoon of coconut butter
- ½ a cup of roasted red pepper chopped up
- 1 large sized finely chopped shallots
- 1 teaspoon of celery salt
- 1 tablespoon of seasoned salt
- 1 teaspoon of organic paprika
- 1 pinch of crushed red pepper flakes
- 4-5 cups of Cauliflower broken up into florets
- 4 cup of vegetable broth
- Just a splash of apple cider vinegar
- 1 pinch fresh thyme
- 1 cup of organic coconut milk

Instructions

Take a heavy bottomed pot and add coconut oil over medium heat. Add chopped up shallots and sauté for 3 minutes. Add chopped up and roasted pepper alongside the seasonings. Stir well and cook for 2-3 minutes. Add cauliflower, fresh thyme and stock

Bring it to a simmer and cover the pot, cook for 5-10 minutes. Work in small batches and puree the soup using an immersion blender. Bring back the whole blended soup back to your pot and stir in coconut milk. Enjoy!

Nutritional Information per Serving

Calories: 221; Total Fat: 17 g; Carbs: 11 g; Dietary Fiber: 1 g;
Protein: 8 g; Cholesterol: 13 mg; Sodium: 705 mg

Chapter 33: Day 30 Meals

BREAKFAST - MINI SANTÉ FE FRITTATAS

Yield: 12 Servings
Total Time: 35 Minutes
Prep Time: 10 Minutes
Cook Time: 25 Minutes

Ingredients:
- Pork sausage: 8 ounces
- Diced yellow and red pepper: 2 cups
- Protein Eggs: 10
- Milk: ½ cup
- Egg whites: 2
- Salt: ½ teaspoon
- Black pepper: ¼ teaspoon
- Pepper jack cheese: ½ cup
- Chopped cilantro: 2 tablespoons

Instructions:
Preheat your oven to 350 degrees Fahrenheit. Cook your sausage in a skillet until it turns golden brown. Remove the fried sausage and in the same skillet fry the diced yellow and red peppers until they are softened. In another bowl, whisk the eggs, milk and the egg whites. Divide the sausage and the fried peppers in to the muffin cups. Now very carefully and evenly pour over the egg mixture on top and put a tablespoon of cheese in every muffin case. Using a fork stir the mixture and then put the muffin tray to bake in the oven for 20 to 25 minutes or until done. Serve!

Nutritional Information per Serving
Calories: 169; Total Fat: 11.2 g; Carbs: 2.8 g; Dietary Fiber: 3 g;
Protein: 11.9 g; Cholesterol: 100 mg; Sodium: 426 mg

LUNCH - WHITE PIZZA FRITTATA

Yield: 10
Total Time: 40 minutes
Prep Time: 10 minutes
Cooking Time: 30 minutes

Ingredients
- 12 large sized eggs
- 9 ounces of Frozen Spinach
- 1 ounce of pepperoni
- 5 ounces of Mozzarella Cheese
- 1 teaspoon of Minced up Garlic
- ½ a cup of parmesan Cheese
- 4 tablespoons of Olive Oil
- ¼ teaspoon of Nutmeg
- Salt as needed
- Pepper as needed

Instructions
Microwave the frozen spinach for 3-4 minutes. Squeeze the spinach later on to drain water out.Pre-heat your oven to 375-degree Fahrenheit. Take a bowl and add eggs, spices and olive oil. Add spinach, ricotta and parmesan. Take an iron skillet and pour the prepared mixture. Sprinkle mozzarella cheese and pepperoni on top
Place it in your oven and bake for 30 minutes. Enjoy!

Nutritional Information per Serving
Calories: 306; Total Fat: 22 g; Carbs: 8 g; Dietary Fiber: 1 g;
Protein: 19 g; Cholesterol: 304 mg; Sodium: 607 mg

DINNER - SPICY RED COCONUT CURRY

Yield: 4
Total Time: 35 minutes
Prep Time: 10 minutes
Cooking Time: 25 minutes

Ingredients
- 1 cup of broccoli florets
- 1 large sized handful of spinach
- 4 tablespoon of coconut oil
- ¼ medium onion
- 1 teaspoon of minced garlic
- 1 teaspoon of minced ginger
- 2 teaspoons of Tamari
- 1 tablespoon of red curry paste
- ½ a cup of coconut cream
- 2 teaspoons of special sauce

Special Sauce:
- 1 and da ½ cup of shredded sea weed
- 6 cups of water
- 6 fat clove garlic crushed but not peeled
- 1 tablespoon of peppercorns
- 1 cup of mushroom Tamari
- 1 tablespoon of miso

Instructions
Take a large saucepan and add garlic, Wakame, pepper corns and water and bring to a boil. Lower down heat and simmer for 20 minutes. Strain and return the liquid to the pot. Add Tamari and bring to a boil again and cook it is very salty. Remove the heat and stir in miso. This is your special sauce. Chop up your onion and mince garlic.
Take a pan and place it over medium-high heat, add chopped up onions and minced garlic.

Add 2 tablespoon of coconut oil and cook until translucent. Turn the heat down to medium-low and add broccoli to pan, stir well. Once the broccolis are cooked, move the veggies on the side and add curry paste. Cook for 60 seconds. Add spinach and top and cook until wilt, add coconut cream alongside the remaining coconut oil.

Stir and add Tamari, special sauce, ginger and allow it to simmer for 10 minutes more

Enjoy!

Nutritional Information per Serving
Calories: 491; Total Fat: 12 g; Carbs: 20 g; Dietary Fiber: 2 g;

Protein: 69 g; Cholesterol: 228 mg;

Sodium: 1621 mg

Conclusion

You did it! Congrats on getting all the way to the end of our Keto Meal Prep Cookbook: 30-Days Meal Prep Guide to Make Delicious and Easy Ketogenic Recipes for A Rapid Weight Loss! This was indeed your very first hurdle to becoming a master of creating delicious Keto meal plans for months to come and is just the first hurdle of many that you will have to overcome on this exciting Keto journey.

I hope you have enjoyed all 90 delicious Keto Meal Plan recipes, and that even after these initial 30 days the recipes will inspire you to mix, match and even come up with your very own.

What happens next?

The next step is to continue practicing and enjoying the recipes as you see fit. Then when you are ready to begin another adventure join us again on yet another one of our amazing culinary journeys. Remember to leave us a positive review if you liked what you read.

Until next time, keep on cooking. Best of luck!

Lightning Source UK Ltd.
Milton Keynes UK
UKHW020639240620
365480UK00010B/442/J